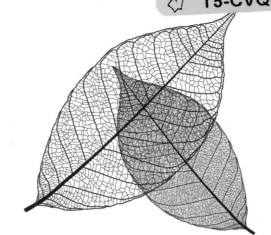

Govern**Green**

Driving Your Organization's
Commitment to Sustainability

Peter A. Soyka   WITHDRAWN

BOARD**SOURCE**®
Building Effective Nonprofit Boards

Library of Congress Cataloging-in-Publication Data

Soyka, Peter Arnim, 1958-

Govern green : driving your organization's commitment to
sustainability / by Peter A. Soyka.

p. cm.

ISBN 1-58686-127-1

1. Nonprofit organizations--Management. 2. Management--
Environmental aspects. 3. Environmentalism. I. Title.

HD62.6.S69 2011

658.4'083--dc23

2011035067

© 2011 BoardSource.
First Printing, September 2011
ISBN 1-58686-127-1

Published by BoardSource
750 9th Street, NW, Suite 650
Washington, DC 20001

The views in each BoardSource publication are those of its author,
and do not represent official positions of BoardSource or its
sponsoring organizations. Information and guidance in this book is
provided with the understanding that BoardSource is not engaged in
rendering professional opinions. If such opinions are required, the
services of an attorney should be sought.

BOARDSOURCE®
Building Effective Nonprofit Boards

BoardSource is dedicated to advancing the public good by building exceptional nonprofit boards and inspiring board service.

BoardSource was established in 1988 by the Association of Governing Boards of Universities and Colleges (AGB) and Independent Sector (IS). Prior to this, in the early 1980s, the two organizations had conducted a survey and found that although 30 percent of respondents believed they were doing a good job of board education and training, the rest of the respondents reported little, if any, activity in strengthening governance. As a result, AGB and IS proposed the creation of a new organization whose mission would be to increase the effectiveness of nonprofit boards.

With a lead grant from the Kellogg Foundation and funding from five other donors, BoardSource opened its doors in 1988 as the National Center for Nonprofit Boards with a staff of three and an operating budget of $385,000. On January 1, 2002, BoardSource took on its new name and identity. These changes were the culmination of an extensive process of understanding how we were perceived, what our audiences wanted, and how we could best meet the needs of nonprofit organizations.

Today, BoardSource is the premier voice of nonprofit governance. Its highly acclaimed products, programs, and services mobilize boards so that organizations fulfill their missions, achieve their goals, increase their impact, and extend their influence. BoardSource is a 501(c)(3) organization.

BoardSource provides

- resources to nonprofit leaders through workshops, training, and an extensive Web site (www.boardsource.org)

- governance consultants who work directly with nonprofit leaders to design specialized solutions to meet an organization's needs

- the world's largest, most comprehensive selection of material on nonprofit governance, including a large selection of books and CD-ROMs

- an annual conference that brings together approximately 900 governance experts, board members, and chief executives and senior staff from around the world

For more information, please visit our Web site at www.boardsource.org, e-mail us at mail@boardsource.org, or call us at 800-883-6262.

Have You Used These BoardSource Resources?

PUBLICATIONS

The Nonprofit Policy Sampler, Second Edition

The Nonprofit Dashboard: A Tool for Tracking Progress

Managing Conflicts of Interest: A Primer for Nonprofit Boards, Second Edition

The Nonprofit Chief Executive's Ten Basic Responsibilities

Chief Executive Transitions: How to Hire and Support a Nonprofit CEO

Assessment of the Chief Executive

The Board Chair Handbook, Second Edition

Building the Governance Partnership: The Chief Executive's Guide to Getting the Best from the Board, Second Edition

Moving Beyond Founder's Syndrome to Nonprofit Success

The Source: Twelve Principles of Governance That Power Exceptional Boards

Exceptional Board Practices: The Source in Action

Navigating the Organizational Lifecycle: A Capacity-Building Guide for Nonprofit Leaders

Generating Buzz: Strategic Communications for Nonprofit Boards

Understanding Nonprofit Financial Statements, Third Edition

The Board Building Cycle: Nine Steps to Finding, Recruiting, and Engaging Nonprofit Board Members, Second Edition

Culture of Inquiry: Healthy Debate in the Boardroom

Chief Executive Succession Planning: Essential Guidance for Boards and CEOs, Second Edition

THE GOVERNANCE SERIES

1. *Ten Basic Responsibilities of Nonprofit Boards, Second Edition*
2. *Legal Responsibilities of Nonprofit Boards, Second Edition*
3. *Financial Responsibilities of Nonprofit Boards, Second Edition*
4. *Fundraising Responsibilities of Nonprofit Boards, Second Edition*
5. *The Nonprofit Board's Role in Mission, Planning, and Evaluation, Second Edition*
6. *Structures and Practices of Nonprofit Boards, Second Edition*

DVDs

Meeting the Challenge: An Orientation to Nonprofit Board Service

Speaking of Money: A Guide to Fundraising for Nonprofit Board Members

ONLINE ASSESSMENTS

Board Self-Assessment

Assessment of the Chief Executive

Executive Search — Needs Assessment

For an up-to-date list of publications and information about current prices, membership, and other services, please call BoardSource at 800-883-6262 or visit our Web site at www.boardsource.org. For consulting services, please e-mail us at consulting@boardsource.org or call 877-892-6293.

CONTENTS

INTRODUCTION

Whether you are a devoted environmentalist with a lifestyle to match, or you believe that the earth and its resources exist for humans to use as they choose, the inescapable fact is that we depend on the natural environment for the resources and materials we need to sustain us and our quality of life. Most readers of this book have had advantages that would have been difficult to imagine a century ago: Our educational experiences, material standard of living, and professional and cultural opportunities greatly exceed those available to the majority of people in our parents' and grandparents' generation. But the benefits that many take for granted in advanced economies have come at a significant cost.

While ambient environmental quality in the United States has improved markedly in recent decades, on a global scale human activity is threatening our most fundamental resources. Given current and projected patterns of consumption and use, it is uncertain whether many amenities we take for granted — such as adequate potable water, flood control, crop pollination, and availability of fish and game — will continue without interruption. Our environment is under siege.

Nonprofit organizations are driven by the mission to serve a social purpose, a cause, or a constituency. Especially in challenging economic times, they must manage scarce resources while keeping a single-minded focus on making a difference by fulfilling their missions. It makes sense for nonprofits to embrace another form of responsibility to their stakeholders and society at large: to assess and commit to reducing their impact on the environment. Whether or not your organization generates substantial waste, pollution, or other obvious environmental aspects, the board and staff leaders should take reasonable steps to improve its environmental posture and performance. With astute leadership, this responsible approach may reveal additional value your organization can offer, such as new or enhanced services to clients or members, or cost savings, operational efficiency, improved staff morale and productivity, or other business-oriented benefits.

This book will help nonprofit boards explore why and how the environment and related matters should be part of their agendas. It is written for board members who understand their governance roles but may not have extensive knowledge of environmental issues in the nonprofit context. In the chapters that follow, I outline some of the major environmental challenges and broader sustainability issues that we face as a society and suggest a role for nonprofit boards in combining effective governance with environmental responsibility.

Part I provides the context for sustainability policies and practices in a nonprofit organization. Chapter 1 reviews the global environmental challenges that are reaching crisis proportions, provides a capsule history of response to environmental issues, and introduces the concept of sustainability. Chapter 2 describes what it takes to create an organization fully capable of implementing sustainability practictes and explains the barriers that typically exist.

Part II addresses the fundamentals of governing green. Chapter 3 lists appropriate points for board involvement: defining the nature of the organization's relationship with the environment, formulating a vision and strategy, developing a sustainability policy, assessing environmental effects, reviewing investments, and providing oversight. To give board members a sense of what's involved at the policy and operational levels, chapter 4 reviews relevant areas for sustainability initiatives in nonprofit organizations.

A NOTE ABOUT TERMINOLOGY

Increasingly, many leading businesses, higher education institutions, nonprofit organizations, and even many environmental advocacy groups are approaching environmental issues through the broad framework of sustainability. Stand-alone approaches focusing only on environmental performance improvement (for example, reducing waste generation or pollutant emissions) are increasingly being abandoned in favor of a construct that is more holistic and, for nonprofit organizations in particular, a more natural fit.

The concept of sustainability emerged from the environmental movement and often is focused on key environmental issues and challenges, but it also encompasses opportunities for nonprofit leaders to examine social equity and economic issues in combination with the environmental aspects of their organizations.

Sustainability, in my view, is a value set, philosophy, and approach rooted in three beliefs:

- that organizations (nonprofit and otherwise) can and must contribute materially to the betterment of society

- that successful organizations must balance their needs, aspirations, and limitations against the larger interests of the societies in which they operate

- that these organizations will be rewarded with loyalty, opportunity, stability, and durable competitive advantage

In this book I use sustainability, rather than greening or environmental improvement, as the key objective to be pursued. Greening sounds and feels admirable, but when economic conditions deteriorate greening programs tend to be jettisoned or scaled back. Sustainability provides the only theoretical and practical environmental improvement framework that can be fully justified and maintained during both good and challenging economic times.

Use of the term green is in vogue, but you should also be aware that organizations must be careful about any claims that they make about their activities and offerings. Terms such as green, carbon neutral, and environmentally preferred are regulated by the U.S. Federal Trade Commission and must be supported with facts and analysis. If you want to learn more about environmental claims and their use, visit www.ftc.gov.

WHY ORGANIZATIONS NEED BOARD LEADERSHIP

To many people, protecting the environment is a civic duty. It may be less obvious, however, why nonprofit boards should concern themselves with this issue, given the diversity of their responsibilities and the challenges inherent in fulfilling them.

Whether your organization is a soup kitchen, an art museum, a child care center, or a wildlife conservation group, it all starts with "governing green": a commitment on the part of board members to rethink fundamental policies and practices that affect the environment, either directly or indirectly. You may find that in improving your environmental performance, you also improve operational efficiency, reduce costs, raise employee morale, or benefit from a socially responsible image. Or you may believe that when it comes to this urgent global issue, it's quite simply the right thing to do.

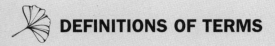
DEFINITIONS OF TERMS

carbon footprint. An organization's total annual emissions of all greenhouse gases, generally expressed in terms of carbon dioxide equivalents (CO_2-e). Carbon, in fully oxidized form (as CO_2) is by far the most important contributor to total greenhouse gas emissions worldwide and for most organizations. *(See also greenhouse gas.)*

corporate social responsibility (CSR). A self-regulating mechanism in which a business monitors and ensures its active compliance with the spirit of the law, ethical standards, and international norms. Acceptance of CSR implies making a positive overall impact on the environment, consumers, employees, communities, and other stakeholders. CSR-focused organizations proactively promote the public interest by encouraging community growth and development and voluntarily eliminate practices that could harm the public, regardless of their legality. CSR and sustainability have common elements, but CSR emphasizes obligations to society, while sustainability, as defined here, equally emphasizes opportunity.

environmental aspect. Element of an organization's activities, products, or services that can interact with the environment. A significant environmental aspect has or can have a significant environmental impact.

environmental footprint. As originally defined, the area of land (e.g., in acres) required to produce all of the resources used by one person in one year. In common (and imprecise) usage, the total environmental burden imposed by a person, organization, or society.

environmental impact. Any change to the environment, whether adverse or beneficial, resulting wholly or partially from an organization's environmental aspects; the effect of an environmental aspect.

environmental, social, and governance (ESG). The current formulation by which many investors evaluate the risks and opportunities presented by investments in particular companies. A category of investor that makes use of corporate sustainability information when making investment decisions.

greenhouse gas (GHG). A gaseous substance that promotes atmospheric warming by trapping heat, thereby contributing to global climate change. Major greenhouse gases include the combustion gases carbon dioxide (CO_2), methane (CH_4), and nitrous oxide (N_2O), as well as the industrial chemicals sulfur hexafluoride, hydrofluorocarbons, and perfluorocarbons. (*See also carbon footprint.*)

sustainability. A value set, philosophy, and approach rooted in the belief that (1) organizations (nonprofit and otherwise) can and must materially contribute to the betterment of society; (2) successful organizations must balance their needs, aspirations, and limitations against the larger interests of the societies in which they operate; and (3) those that do will be rewarded with loyalty, opportunity, stability, and durable competitive advantage.

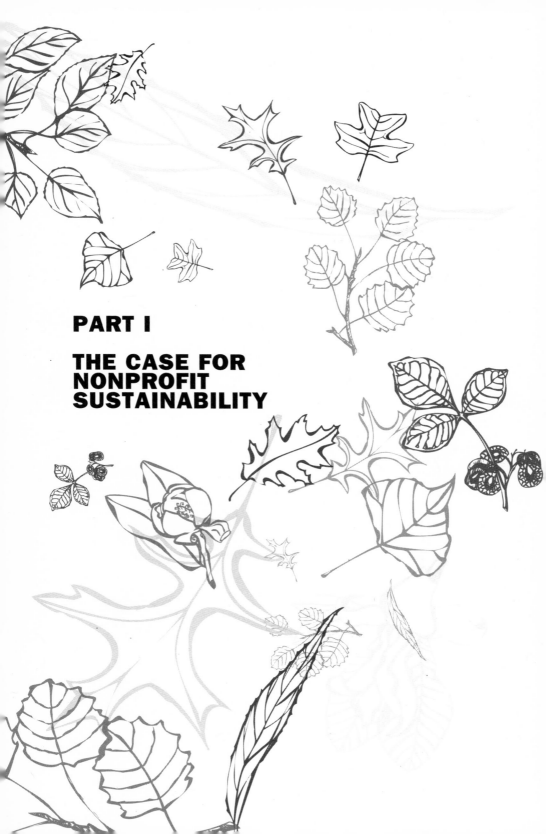

PART I

THE CASE FOR NONPROFIT SUSTAINABILITY

Chapter 1

Protecting the Environment: A New Component of the Nonprofit Mission

In less than two generations, there has been a sea change in attitudes toward global environmental problems. Nearly everyone wants to have a healthy environment, and many feel obligated to contribute to this goal. We also expect corporations and other institutions to conduct their affairs in a way that does not impose undue burdens on the environment and that complies with all pertinent environmental regulations. Our understanding of what environmental protection involves, whom it affects, and who actively participates has reached a new level of sophistication over the past four decades.

Along many fronts, however, we face an environmental crisis that requires clear thinking, hard work, and determination to overcome. Although the challenging but conceptually more straightforward work of limiting waste and pollution sources is under way, the remaining threats to human health and the quality of our environment are more subtle, diffuse, and under the influence of many more people than those we have engaged so far.

As a reminder of the urgency of this global imperative, think about the everyday behavior of most Americans. We drive cars or trucks on a daily basis, and we tend to work at some distance from our homes. Walking, biking, carpooling, and public transportation remain impractical or time consuming for most people. Although emission controls are improving, people are driving more. We live in larger homes and consume goods and services more freely than we did even a decade ago. All of these behaviors, which fundamentally reflect lifestyle choices, have created a nation of prodigious energy consumers. By consuming so much energy, we generate significant, ongoing pollutant emissions and create the need for substantial oil imports, posing both economic and national security concerns.

The way forward — and the only way forward — is for each of us to accept personal responsibility for the choices we make in our daily lives and take reasonable steps to limit or reduce the adverse impacts that our choices may have on the environment and its long-term capacity to meet our needs. Those in leadership positions in organizations of all kinds — corporations, government agencies, and nonprofits — have a similar obligation to understand and take reasonable steps to control the adverse impacts of their organizations' activities on environmental quality.

HUMAN IMPACT: A SHORT HISTORY

Since the dawn of humankind, people have used resources from the natural world and affected their surroundings through their activities. Until the modern age, human impact on the environment was limited in magnitude and geographic scale; for example, hunting and fishing depleted the population of game animals or fish in a particular area, or the slash-and-burn techniques of subsistence agriculture contributed to deforestation, soil nutrient loss, erosion, and biodiversity loss in the affected land. The negative consequences of human activity were almost always felt by the people (or their descendants) who overexploited local natural resources, causing migration or, in extreme cases, extinction of a local or regional culture. The long-term impact tended to be limited in terms of the spread of human populations, their overall societal and cultural development, and lasting impacts on the health of the local environment.

These patterns changed markedly with the exponential human population and technological growth during the 20th century. With the rapid and extreme overexploitation of key natural resource stocks — from commercial fisheries to tropical hardwood rain forests — the rate of ongoing species loss has grown markedly. Conservation experts warn that human activity is accelerating the extinction of plants and animals, mainly through habitat loss. Not only have these species' contributions to their local ecosystems been lost, but in most cases so has their genetic material. This means that these organisms' potential as sources of new medicines, crops, and other valuable products will never be available to us.

Human activity is also causing global climate change as greenhouse gas emissions, especially carbon dioxide, accelerate the temperature rise in the earth's atmosphere. Climate change will affect food production, water availability, and the health of ecosystems such as forests and wetlands. It could intensify many environmental and human health problems, cause millions to lose their livelihoods, and lead to conflict over resources. Excessive resource use coupled with the absence of long-range planning and inadequate institutional controls in many parts of the world is threatening ecosystem services such as clean water, flood control, climate regulation, crop pollination, and supplies of timber, nuts, fruits, and other goods. In many areas, these services are vital to local and regional populations and economies and, in some cases — water, for example — they are also necessary for human habitation.

WHAT IS KNOWN ABOUT CLIMATE CHANGE

"Science has made enormous progress toward understanding climate change. As a result, there is a strong, credible body of evidence, based on multiple lines of research, documenting that Earth is warming. Strong evidence also indicates that recent warming is largely caused by human activities, especially the release of greenhouse gases through the burning of fossil fuels. Global warming is closely associated with other climate changes and impacts, including rising sea levels, increases in intense rainfall events, decreases in snow cover and sea ice, more frequent and intense heat waves, increases in wildfires, longer growing seasons, and ocean acidification. Individually and collectively, these changes pose risks for a wide range of human and environmental systems. While much remains to be learned, the core phenomenon, scientific questions, and hypotheses have been examined thoroughly and have stood firm in the face of serious scientific debate and careful evaluation of alternative explanations."

Source: U.S. National Academy of Sciences, America's Climate Choices: Advancing the Science of Climate Change. Report in Brief, 2010.

The continued growth of human populations remains an important driving force behind current challenges to maintaining the quality and health of the environment, and to moving our society and the world to a more sustainable posture. In the United States and in many other developed countries, population growth has slowed during the past couple of decades, but overall populations continue to grow as a function of longer life spans enabled by advances in medicine, the transition to an information economy, higher standards of living, and in some cases, immigration. At the same time, most countries are getting "older." Indeed, in many developed countries, including the United States, the "oldest old" (those 80 and above) is the fastest growing component of the population. In developing countries, in contrast, human populations continue to grow dramatically, due to high birth rates and persistent poverty, and most citizens are younger than 20 years old. Both of these ongoing trends present challenges to societies and regional environments around the world, as greater demands are placed upon younger generations to meet their own needs as well as those of elder citizens in developed countries, and increasing, and unsustainable, pressures are placed upon critical natural resources (e.g., water, arable land, fisheries) in developing countries.

FAST FACTS ABOUT THE STATE OF THE WORLD'S ENVIRONMENT

"The structure and functioning of the world's ecosystems changed more rapidly in the second half of the twentieth century than at any time in human history...

- More land was converted to cropland in the 30 years after 1950 than in the 150 years between 1700 and 1850.

- Approximately 20% of the world's coral reefs were lost and an additional 20% degraded in the last several decades of the twentieth century, and approximately 35% of mangrove area was lost during this time.

- Since 1960, flows of reactive (biologically available) nitrogen in terrestrial ecosystems have doubled, and flows of phosphorus have tripled. More than half of all the synthetic nitrogen fertilizer, which was first manufactured in 1913, ever used on the planet has been used since 1985.

- The number of species on the planet is declining. Over the past few hundred years, humans have increased the species extinction rate by as much as 1,000 times over background rates typical over the planet's history.

- The use of two ecosystem services — capture fisheries and fresh water — is now well beyond levels that can be sustained even at current demands, much less future ones. At least one quarter of important commercial fish stocks are overharvested....Some 15–35% of irrigation withdrawals exceed supply rates and are therefore unsustainable.

- The frequency and impact of floods and fires has increased significantly in the past 50 years, in part due to ecosystem changes....Annual economic losses from extreme events increased tenfold from the 1950s to approximately $70 billion in 2003, of which natural catastrophes (floods, fires, storms, drought, earthquakes) accounted for 84% of insured losses."

Source: Millennium Ecosystem Assessment, Ecosystems and Human Well-Being: Synthesis, World Health Organization, 2005.

OUR NATIONAL RESPONSE

In the United States after World War II, we experienced dramatic population growth and an economic boom that gave rise to some of today's most vexing environmental problems. In this new consumer economy — in part a response to pent-up demand during the war years — people abandoned cities in favor of a more comfortable suburban lifestyle enabled by the automobile and inexpensive (and highly subsidized) petroleum. The principal threats were not terrorism or global climate change but communism and the threat of nuclear war.

The intense social and political turmoil of the mid- to late 1960s had profound effects on our society. Though resolving the issues in play proved challenging — and to some degree remains an ongoing task — it is fair to say that the progress we made has helped our nation become not only more equitable, but more dynamic, politically stable, economically productive, internationally competitive, and sustainable.

From the 1960s, the modern environmental movement emerged. The publication of Rachel Carson's classic *Silent Spring* in 1962 first brought public attention to the issue of pesticides in the environment and to the fact that no one had the authority at that time to limit their production, use, and misuse. Images and stories of environmental crisis began to appear: a New Hampshire river flowing a deep, opaque red from dyes dumped by textile mills; extreme air pollution episodes that sickened and killed people in major cities around the world, including well-conditioned young athletes on their practice fields; and a 1969 fire on the Cuyahoga River in Ohio — not the first but the one that captured public attention.

Beginning with the first Earth Day in 1970, a powerful movement stimulated passage of major laws governing pollutant emissions to air, water, and land and regulating, for the first time, the manufacture and use of pesticides and other toxic chemicals (Exhibit 1.1). These early laws were followed in the mid-1970s and 1980s by new statutes controlling the management of hazardous wastes, mandating the cleanup of uncontrolled hazardous waste sites, establishing controls over drinking water quality, and requiring public disclosure of toxic pollutant emissions. These statutes expanded the federal government's authority — previously limited to public land stewardship and food and drug safety — to encompass the protection of human health and the environment. A number of subsequent laws and treaties enacted addressed specific natural resource management and use issues, without substantially changing the intent or effect of the major environmental control statutes.

Exhibit 1.1

MAJOR U.S. ENVIRONMENTAL LEGISLATION, 1969–2007

1969 National Environmental Policy Act

1970 Clean Air Act

1970 Occupational Safety and Health Act

1972 Noise Control Act

1972 Federal Water Pollution Control Act (Clean Water Act)

1973 Endangered Species Act

1974 Safe Drinking Water Act

1974 Hazardous Materials Transportation Act

1976 Resource Conservation and Recovery Act

1976 Toxic Substances Control Act

1980 Solid Waste Disposal Act

1980 Comprehensive Environmental Response, Compensation, and Liability Act (Superfund)

1990 Oil Pollution Act

1990 Pollution Prevention Act

1993 North American Free Trade Agreement

2003 Healthy Forests Initiative

2005 Energy Policy Act

2007 Energy Independence and Security Act

We have come a long way in 40 years. The regulatory control framework envisioned in the major environmental statutes has been more or less fully completed, and the regular, ongoing oversight and enforcement of these laws and their implementing regulations have now been delegated to state governments in most cases. As a result, uniform, protective standards have been deployed nationwide in a way that reflects each state's characteristics and priorities, allowing for flexible, practical application at the local level. As the new environmental laws (and, in parallel, occupational safety and health laws) were implemented, new processes, operating practices, and capabilities were developed that enabled organizations to greatly reduce their pollutant generation and emission and accident rates.

It is important to celebrate the successes of environmental, health, and safety protection efforts in improving air and water quality; reducing exposure to toxic chemicals; protecting high-value ecosystems and habitats; eliminating death, injuries, and illness on the job; and other areas. Pollution prevention — eliminating pollution at its source rather than relying on downstream treatment or disposal — is strongly preferred by regulators and leading companies and has been U.S. national policy since 1990. Similarly, the field of occupational health and safety has embraced the concept of behavior-based safety since the mid-1990s.

We made progress in the environmental protection arena because conditions were sufficiently dire to enable consensus among Democrats and Republicans, liberals, and conservatives that strong measures needed to be taken. It probably helped that at the time, the specific sources of many major environmental problems were not well understood, nor were the initial costs of more benign practices, some of which turned out to be quite large. In today's political climate, it is far more difficult to move legislation through the gauntlet of the entrenched interests represented in the U.S. Congress. Nevertheless, we have a mature and generally well-functioning legal and regulatory system to define key environmental, health, and safety issues. Given the political realities, it is unlikely that the current system is going to change markedly in the foreseeable future.

WHERE WE ARE NOW

Today, the regulatory, policy, and technical expertise within many public-sector institutions is highly developed, as is the published literature in such fields as environmental and health and safety law, public policy, pollution control engineering, risk assessment, and environmental and natural resource economics. Experience has shown which types of approaches are effective and can be implemented at reasonable cost and which are not or cannot. Private-sector environmental expertise is available from a multibillion-dollar set of industries that collectively employ hundreds of thousands of consultants, engineers, scientists, and other professionals who deliver an array of products and services in the environmental, health and safety, and related fields. And while the basics of managing wastes, controlling pollutant emissions, and limiting unsafe workplace exposures remain ongoing challenges in some operating environments, increasingly the focus is on rethinking and redesigning business processes to make them safer and more environmentally benign rather than on end-of-pipe pollution control.

In initial efforts to improve environmental quality, we tackled the most obvious and most easily addressed problems first. We went after major pollution sources that were in plain sight and generally under the direct control of an entity — a corporation, hospital, or local government, for example — that could be identified and compelled to make the desired changes. These efforts were hugely successful, and contrary to dire predictions, they did not bankrupt our society — or very many, if any, companies. The plain truth is that the vast majority of environmental and health and safety laws have yielded tangible environmental quality, human health, and economic benefits, the value of which — despite what their detractors say — greatly exceeds their costs.

Now we are left with the tough stuff: major environmental issues that continue to defy adequate resolution. They include the following:

- reducing greenhouse gas (GHG) emissions and limiting global climate change

- ensuring adequate water supply and quality

- understanding and limiting the effects of endocrine-disrupting chemicals

- appropriately controlling exposure to low- and no-threshold effect compounds and mixtures

- preventing the spread of invasive species

- reducing line and area sources of pollution, such as roads and farm fields

AREN'T ENVIRONMENTAL REGULATIONS TOO COSTLY?

Studies conducted over nearly 40 years show that well-designed environmental regulations yield significant net societal benefits — that is, they do not cost money; they save money. For example, EPA recently calculated that the overall benefits of the Clean Air Act Amendments of 1990 and their implementation exceeded the associated costs by a factor of more than 30. These benefits will reach $2 trillion by 2020.

Source: U.S. Environmental Protection Agency, Office of Air and Radiation. "The Benefits and Costs of the Clean Air Act: 1990 to 2020 Summary Report," March 2011. www.epa.gov/air/sect812/prospective2.html.

Addressing these challenges adequately — and, at a more personal level, doing what we can within our own spheres of influence — will require better understanding of what the environmental issue is, how performance can be improved, and what the practical and financial consequences of action (or inaction) are at personal, organizational, and societal levels.

These issues are difficult to resolve for some or all of the following situations:

- **Diffuse pollution sources.** Many remaining major pollution sources are scattered rather than centralized (for example, in a power or chemical plant), making them more difficult to control.

- **Large infrastructure investments.** Some environmental issues are intimately associated with our chosen life and work styles and with our commercial and industrial infrastructure — for example, the near-total reliance on petroleum to power our personal mobility and the unabated suburban sprawl that has exacerbated our dependence on the automobile.

- **Individual behavior.** The individual choices we make every day or at periodic intervals affect environmental issues, and they are well beyond the traditional purview of government and, for that matter, most societal institutions.

- **Trans-boundary issues**. Some environmental problems — climate change, for example — span national and other political boundaries, so finding and reaching agreement on solutions can be difficult and time consuming, even if there is general agreement about the source of the problem and what needs to be done.

- **Obsolete, limited authority.** Despite the profound impacts of major environmental statutes, any new environmental improvement efforts that rely on legal controls are limited by the boundaries and approaches established by those statutes. With a few exceptions, these laws are all at least 20 years old.

- **Gridlock**. Profound philosophical differences within political, government, and corporate institutions make it difficult to reach consensus on the nature, causes, desired improvements, and indicated approaches for resolving important environmental and sustainability issues.

When it comes to addressing these tough dilemmas, where do nonprofit organizations fit in? It is clear that environmental and broader sustainability issues are of substantial and growing importance in all sectors of our society. The expectation of good stewardship toward the environment applies to nonprofits as surely as it does profit-oriented corporations. This means that boards and their organizations must exercise vigilance and develop sound policies and approaches to satisfy these evolving expectations. The next chapter explores the implications for boards and describes an essential first step: creating an organizational culture that supports a deep commitment to sustainability and that is capable of implementing any appropriate operational changes.

Chapter 2

Creating the Conditions Needed to Govern Green

Environmental protection, environmental enhancement, and efforts to promote a more sustainable future for all are consistent with the role of nonprofit organizations in American society. Even if your organization's mission has no connection to environmental issues, it is part of a larger nonprofit community grounded in a broad commitment to improving people's lives.

The precise nature of the relationship between aspirations to promote environmental sustainability and the mission of your organization may require some additional clarity, which the board must provide. Similarly, the degree to which the organization and the board can control or even influence its environmental aspects may seem limited, but it should be examined carefully nonetheless.

SOLIDIFYING AN INFORMED, RESPONSIBLE, AND CAPABLE ORGANIZATION

Developing an environmental or sustainability policy and related initiatives is a complex undertaking that also offers substantial rewards. In parallel with broader societal trends, on the environmental front there are many competing voices, as well as abundant information — and misinformation. Sorting through it all can be both time consuming and confusing but is essential. Any new program or initiative addressing sustainability must be built upon facts, not opinion. Active board leadership is absolutely essential. Without it, any new sustainability-oriented initiative is likely to founder or, at best, not reach its full potential.

An essential starting point is a common understanding of and collective commitment to environmental and social responsibility, in which shared values and beliefs guide your organization toward cogent policies and proactive practices. It also is very important to understand and address any structural or cultural issues that might limit understanding and the effectiveness of any new activities to pursue sustainability. Both for-profit and nonprofit entities and their staffs have learned a great deal during the past few decades about how to manage environmental and broader sustainability issues. Their experiences reveal the following fruitful approaches to creating or improving an organization that can both aspire to and achieve sustained improvements in environmental, social, and economic performance:

- **Leading from the top.** With any new initiative, particularly one that involves substantial organizational change, it is vital that senior leadership (the board, chief executive, and other senior staff) be directly and visibly involved and show their ongoing support.

- **Gaining an understanding of the environmental footprint.** Sound policy and effective decision making are based on facts and analysis rather than supposition. Taking the time and investing the resources to truly understand your organization's environmental and social aspects is a key step to defining and carrying out a strategy and program that will produce meaningful results.

- **Determining control and influence.** Many organizations have only limited direct control or influence over certain parts of their environmental footprint — for example, the energy consumption and pollutant emission of the building they occupy. Knowing where and how action works better than persuasion is important to focusing your improvement efforts effectively and efficiently.

- **Interacting with and understanding stakeholders' concerns.** Today, virtually all stakeholders expect to have a voice and to be heard. For most nonprofits, important stakeholders include members, funders, and recipients of services. Including them at some level early in the conversation about sustainability could not only surface important concerns and promising ideas but also limit the possibility that they will raise significant complaints and concerns once the program is under way. As the old saying goes, "An ounce of prevention is worth a pound of cure."

- **Defining clear and appropriate objectives.** For any performance improvement initiative to succeed over the long haul, it must have some goals. Given the vague nature and limited understanding of the environmental footprint within most organizations (even sophisticated corporations), it is important to be specific and realistic about what any new initiative is intended to achieve. Signing on to "save the world" is not going to provide your staff members with the milestones that they will need to guide their actions and monitor progress. Objectives (long-term goals) should be specifically defined and be meaningful but attainable.

- **Evaluating issue and strategy options within mission and cultural context.** Most organizations exist for reasons other than protecting or improving the quality of the environment or maximizing the health and well-being of their employees. Accordingly, any new environmental or sustainability initiative (and implementing internal group or team) must support and invigorate the organization's fundamental purpose, rather than constrain or detract from it.

- **Maintaining cross-functional teams and breaking silos.** In larger organizations, where specialization is more prominent, it is important to ensure that all relevant perspectives are brought to bear in taking on an important new issue or initiative. This is especially true for an issue like environmental management or sustainability, which by nature is multidisciplinary. In companies of significant scale, cross-functional teams are often formed that include representatives of facilities (engineering, maintenance), operations, finance, marketing/development, fulfillment/service delivery, legal, and communications, as well as a representative of senior management. While many nonprofits do not have the scale, degree of specialization, or high-impact environmental aspects to warrant forming a team of this size or complexity, the principle still holds: Assembling a small team with some diversity of membership tends to be more effective than delegating an assignment to one individual, even if that person holds a position of authority.

- **Implementing appropriate policies, strategies, systems, and work practices.** Talking about better environmental performance will not make it happen; rather, it must be driven through structural improvements. This means, at minimum, formal policies and procedures, which provide clear guidance regarding the organization's boundaries for acceptable and expected behavior and how to carry out key tasks to improve performance over time.

- **Monitoring, measuring, reporting, and continually improving.** We manage what we measure, and to know how we're doing, ongoing measurements and occasional course corrections are essential. Performance metrics and timetables should reflect meaningful advances in performance, be challenging but realistic, and be appropriate to the organization's principal business lines and scale.

In chapters 3 and 4, I elaborate on how all of these principles can be applied in the context of helping to put your organization on the path toward environmental/health performance improvement and long-term sustainability.

BOARD READINESS QUIZ

1. Do you believe that the nonprofit sector has the knowledge, skill sets, resources, and overall capability to contribute to solving our society's sustainability challenges?

2. Do you believe that your organization and the people within it have the passion, capability, determination, and drive required to develop and deploy a successful sustainability initiative or program?

3. Do you believe that, as a board member, you can provide the necessary leadership to such a venture?

4. Do you believe that such an initiative or program would make a material difference and be a wise use of time and resources?

5. Do you believe that you can make a convincing case before your fellow board members and the chief executive that your organization should at least explore the development and deployment of a sustainability initiative or program?

If your answer to all of these questions is "yes," then your choice is clear. If your answer to any of the questions is "no," then consider starting small until the board and the organization gain the confidence that pursuing greater sustainability is of value.

BARRIERS TO ORGANIZATIONAL CHANGE

Embracing sustainability means instituting at least some degree of organizational change. Assuming that a policy is in place to guide change and your board is fulfilling its governance and oversight roles (see Chapter 3), four factors can limit the pace and effectiveness of efforts to move your organization toward addressing environmental and broader sustainability issues:

- resistance to change

- lack of personal incentive on the part of staff

- a low level of environmental literacy within the organization

- a decentralized or uncoordinated approach to sustainability initiatives

A strong working relationship between the board and the chief executive is essential to recognize and overcome these barriers to success. As the line manager responsible for the staff and their activities and accomplishments, the chief executive must be aware of these factors and take steps to prevent or counteract them. The board should provide any necessary support and encouragement for the chief executive to address these and any other issues that might limit the organization's progress toward attaining its sustainability goals.

RESISTANCE TO CHANGE

Many organizations have a well-established way of doing things and may not welcome change or promote individual initiative. Those who would suggest a new or better way may have a high burden of proof to surmount, and if they are relatively early in their careers — and have not come of age professionally in the culture and work practices of their employer — they may be accepting significant risk by challenging the existing order, even if at the margins. Questioning the wisdom of the existing hierarchy could be considered a career-limiting move. Board members and the chief executive together can do a lot to ensure that they project and, as appropriate, enforce an attitude of openness to productive change, challenges to the status quo, and, in general, suggestions and feedback from staff at all levels. Those who are closest to the issues often have the best vantage point for seeing what works and what could be improved.

PERSONAL INCENTIVE

Sometimes the personal incentives for staff members are not fully aligned with those of the organization. For example, there may be established goals for recycling paper and other solid wastes that apply to all employees. But if staff who are responsible for doing the work — collecting, sorting, and managing materials to be recycled — perceive it as extra steps in their already-full workday with no extra benefits or recognition, then they are not likely to be enthusiastic about the recycling initiative. No board member should be surprised that such arrangements tend to produce little in the way of results, other than, perhaps, more disgruntled employees. The key is to ensure that the incentives for the staff and the organization are aligned. Most people simply like to feel that their extra effort is valued, and a reward in the form of recognition, workplace amenities, or spot bonuses can go a long way toward stimulating the type of behavioral change that may be desired.

ENVIRONMENTAL LITERACY

Research shows that environmental literacy among American adults is quite low. Most people — regardless of age, income, or education — do not understand basic concepts of environmental science. More fundamentally, science literacy in general is limited, and according to assessments of elementary and secondary students, the level of achievement in science is declining. This is a persistent and serious problem that affects the capability of staff in organizations to understand and take appropriate action on environmental/sustainability issues. To get and keep a sustainability program on track, many organizations provide initial training on environmental/sustainability basics, issues that are most likely to be important to the organization, effective response strategies, and other topics. Another common technique is to provide ongoing "brown bag" or other seminars on sustainability-oriented topics of interest. In larger organizations, inviting guest speakers to share information and perspectives also may be a good way in which to both promote understanding and awareness and maintain enthusiasm among the staff.

DECENTRALIZED MANAGEMENT

Some organizations have a culture and tradition of decentralized management, which may pose some challenges when trying to achieve a consistent and effective approach to improving performance. Regardless of an organization's usual approach, change in pursuit of sustainability must be guided by sound policy, clear lines of authority, and a coordinated internal approach to achieving goals. The board, chief executive, and senior staff set the tone. Without a cohesive, organization-wide commitment, staff members may be left to implement a sustainability initiative on their own. Their efforts can be scattered, and tangible performance improvement by the organization as a whole is diminished. The board and chief executive need to ensure that the organization speaks with one voice, through senior leadership; has decided on specific tactics for achieving goals; and has defined metrics for measuring outcomes against expectations.

EXTERNAL CHALLENGES

For organizations that decide to take on the environmental/ sustainability issue and improve their performance, there are external challenges as well. As public concern about the environment increases, stakeholders and others have growing expectations for organizations of all kinds. These expectations can create particular challenges for organizations such as nonprofits, which have never been subject to significant environmental or health and safety regulations or other requirements. Among other challenges, the organization may have limited existing internal knowledge of its environmental footprint and lack the internal expertise needed to determine its environmental and health and safety aspects. In contemplating a new strategy or program, the organization's leadership also must work through the process of defining the relationship of environmental and related issues to its mission and operations, which may not be obvious. A related issue is that many organizations have only limited control and influence over their environmental and human health aspects. For example, an organization's most significant aspects may be energy use and pollutant emissions from operating its building (or portion thereof). If the building space is leased, the organization may never or only rarely receive information that would allow it to quantify its environmental aspects and might have very little ability to change building operations in a way that would reduce these aspects.

Finally, any evaluation of the organization's current posture and future goals and plans may be affected by many competing voices and by information (or misinformation) from various interested parties. Sorting out competing perspectives, separating fact from fiction, and reaching definitive conclusions can require significant effort and mental discipline. Doing so is vital to reaching appropriate decisions that are focused on the most important issues and make best use of the organization's resources. Boards should provide clear direction and ongoing guidance to the chief executive and staff as a sustainability program takes shape.

STRENGTHENING CAPABILITY STARTS WITH THE BOARD

Build a board with knowledge and ability that's a model for your organization.

- **Get organized.** Appoint a small task force, or ask an interested board member to serve as the board's point person on environmental/sustainability matters.

- **Commit resources.** Beginning with the environmental aspects assessment, the organization needs to budget for sustainability.

- **Learn more.** Invite an expert on corporate or organizational environmental responsibility to speak at a board meeting.

- **Take a field trip.** Visit an organization with a well-developed sustainability policy and practices.

- **Capitalize on board talent.** Find out whether board members have experience with sustainability initiatives in the businesses or organizations where they work.

PART II

GOVERNING GREEN:
MAKING IT HAPPEN

Chapter 3

Leading Sustainability

As keepers of an organization's mission, the board determines what programs and initiatives, among many priorities and needs, are both consistent with the mission and make financial sense. Given competing demands and resource limitations, the board must be very circumspect in considering whether and under what circumstances it might wish to become involved in something new, particularly if the new venture is complex and may appear to have only a very limited connection to the mission.

When it comes to sustainability, the leadership of nonprofit organizations can effectively leverage its talents and limited time by focusing on the roles and responsibilities that boards and board members are uniquely qualified to fulfill:

- defining the nature of the organization's relationship with the environment

- formulating a vision and strategy

- developing a sustainability policy

- assessing environmental effects

- reviewing investments

- providing oversight

DEFINING THE NATURE OF THE ORGANIZATION'S RELATIONSHIP WITH THE ENVIRONMENT

The first and perhaps most important board role is to evaluate environmental issues within the context of your organization's mission, vision, and values. The extent to which environmental protection and enhancement are consistent with, support, or advance the organization's reasons for being should define the degree to which you view environmental activities as opportunities or as obligations. The distinction is vital, and your organization's posture on this point will flow through all subsequent decisions and activities, even if only implicitly. The board should take a clear position on this question very early in the development of any new sustainability initiative.

With the notable exception of organizations whose missions involve the environment, health and safety, sustainability, or any of their components, most nonprofit organizations will not view environmental performance improvement as a direct opportunity to fulfill their goals. From a broader perspective, however, many nonprofits are involved in work that has clear ties to the concept of sustainability. These organizations have the ability not only to reduce their adverse environmental or human health impacts but also to induce improvements in the wider communities in which they operate. Consider the following examples.

Housing and community development advocacy organizations. These organizations are attempting to improve opportunities and quality of life for poor and disadvantaged people, often in urban areas but also in rural communities and on Indian reservations. They can address the direct environmental and human health hazards in substandard housing, such as exposure to lead paint, asbestos, mold, and unsafe drinking water. Another common threat in many disadvantaged communities is high exposure to diesel exhaust from heavy truck traffic, which is a toxic air pollutant and likely human carcinogen. In addition, organizations involved in building or renovating residential and community space have many opportunities to use energy-efficient and other green building components, which reduce both emissions and costs for community residents.

Educational, religious, and cultural institutions. Schools, churches, museums, and other institutions that own and operate buildings of significant size or number have an array of environmental issues. Some may have formal environmental programs, or at least be required to obtain permits (for example, an air emissions permit for a boiler). These organizations have an opportunity to consider their environmental footprint in the broader context of sustainability, which may help them find more ways to contribute to their mission and other societal improvements. Educational institutions, for example, have a clear opportunity to help narrow the significant knowledge and capability gap concerning environmental and sustainability issues. Many colleges and universities have large-scale initiatives to improve their environmental performance. The most effective of these sustainability programs begin with board-endorsed policies and master plans, include responsible analysis of investment priorities, and provide an infrastructure to support an institution-wide effort that engages faculty, staff, and students. Board-level leadership, dedicated administrative capability, and faculty buy-in are essential.

Health care institutions. Hospitals and other health care facilities have many of the same physical plant characteristics as educational institutions, with the additional complexities of dealing with infectious and biohazardous materials, radioactive and/or hazardous reagents and other chemicals, and a host of other environmental health and safety issues. In addition, their mission of protecting, restoring, and improving human health gives them a unique opportunity to focus on policies, practices, and initiatives to improve the health of their patients and other people in their communities while protecting their employees' well-being. Boards of health care facilities may wish to establish more comprehensive policies and plans that expand on the largely tactical activities of managing building energy use and waste materials.

Foundations, endowments, and pension funds. These organizations' principal activity is investing money, either in other nonprofit activity or, in the case of pension funds, in financial and real assets to generate earnings for the benefit of particular groups of people. They have numerous opportunities to apply sustainability principles to their ongoing business activities, from environmentally responsible investing to ensuring that grant recipients have adopted certain policies and practices. This practice is similar to policies of major commercial banks, most of which endorse the Equator Principles as guidelines for managing social and environmental issues related to the financing of economic development programs in less-developed countries (www.equator-principles.com).

In many nonprofits, particularly small ones, there will be limited opportunity to move the needle substantially on environmental or broader sustainability issues. These issues can reasonably be viewed as constraints rather than opportunities, with their management taking the form of policies and practices designed to limit adverse impact rather than capture new opportunities for broad-scale improvement.

RESPONSIBLE INVESTING

United Church Funds (UCF) offers investors the unique opportunity to align their values with their desire to maximize endowment and other assets, believing solid returns can coexist with socially responsible investing (SRI), which is managed through UCF's office of Corporate Social Responsibility (CSR). Social screens offer a starting point for UCF's SRI strategy, establishing the percentage of revenue a corporation may derive from particular products or services before its stock may no longer be held by UCF —

Alcohol	**10%**
Gambling	**10%**
Tobacco	**1%**
Conventional weapons	**10%**
Nuclear weapons	**5%**

More than simply screening-out selected investments, however, United Church Funds engages in active shareholder collaboration with ecumenical partners and the Interfaith Center for Corporate Responsibility. In addition to voting proxies in a manner that reflects UCC values around issues of human health and dignity, environmental integrity and moral responsibility, UCF often joins other investors in advancing shareholder resolutions, such as those demanding greater transparency in corporate governance. UCF also seeks to comply with General Synod resolutions that call on the church to use its economic power to promote justice and peace.

Source: United Church Foundation. http://unitedchurchfunds.org/

THE PACKARD FOUNDATION'S COMMITMENT TO SUSTAINABILITY

This excerpt from The David and Lucile Packard Foundation's sustainability policy explains why its grantmaking and operational values are connected.

From its inception, The David and Lucile Packard Foundation has been focused on promoting sustainability as part of its grantmaking and day-to-day operations. Our Conservation and Science program directly explores the links between action and ideas to help conserve and protect natural systems in the United States and around the world. From our support of efforts to slow climate change, to our partnerships with organizations to protect and restore threatened species, our grantmaking programs are committed to finding long-term solutions for some of our most vexing environmental problems.

Similarly, our commitment to sustainability extends to our Foundation's operations and to ensuring that we conduct our business in ways that will help promote the conservation of our environment and preserve our resources for generations to come. We believe that we can best serve our grantees and the communities we support by living the values that we espouse in our grantmaking, and by taking steps to minimize our impact on our natural world.

FORMULATING A VISION AND STRATEGY

Before embarking upon any sustainability initiative, the board should view environmental and social issues through the lens of the organization's basic reason for being: its mission, vision for the future, objectives and commitments, and strategy. Many boards and staffs begin with an examination of specific environmental and social issues and how they can be managed more efficiently and effectively. While certainly it is important to remain responsive to immediate stakeholder concerns and unexpected events, a better approach is to look at the big picture first. I strongly encourage a vision and strategy that are appropriate to the nature of the enterprise. Begin with your organization's mission, core values, long-range objectives, and strategy, and set the tactical environmental and social issues of the day into this broad framework.

A top-down approach to shaping a vision for a sustainability initiative provides an opportunity to identify the issues that speak to or are aligned with core operational matters and to develop an early sense of their relative magnitude in comparison with other large-scale organizational issues. It is far more effective than trying to divine or distill overall principles out of a bottom-up synthesis of the organization's perceived environmental or stakeholder issues. At the very least, implementing this approach helps ensure that the sustainability strategy and its implementing structures and activities are in harmony with the overall direction of the organization and therefore more likely to be embraced by its members and other stakeholders.

This approach also may help to illuminate more subtle trends that could have significant impact on the organization in the future. One thing that drops out of such an analysis is the environmental and social issues that may pose the biggest opportunities and threats to the organization and are worthy of further evaluation. (Note that the same issue may offer opportunities in some areas and pose threats in others or do so under an alternate set of conditions.)

With a vision in place, a coherent and comprehensive strategy comes next. Strategy is the coordinated set of actions that (along with an environmental or sustainability policy) guide a sustainability program or initiative. Without a well-articulated strategy, goal setting and improvement programs are likely to be misdirected or, at best, not reach their full potential. The sustainability strategy must be an organic extension of the overall organizational strategy. It should be based on the organization's mission, vision, and business culture as well as an informed understanding of the interests of its stakeholders.

For nonprofit organizations, effectiveness in achieving mission, financial stability, and predictability are appropriate objectives, particularly in light of the recent financial crisis and recession and its lasting effects on charitable giving and the financial posture and prospects of many nonprofits. The strategy should be feasible to implement and not impose unnecessary financial stress on the organization.

EXAMPLES OF VISION AND STRATEGY

A few illustrations of developing a sustainability vision and strategy in the nonprofit context follow. In these cases, components of the stand-alone sustainability strategy have elements that dovetail with the organization's mission and existing core activities.

Food banks, soup kitchens, homeless shelters, and other organizations providing sustenance. Consider expanding the existing vision to include developing basic life skills and self-reliance as a means of promoting individual and community sustainability. The strategy could include finding ways to reduce the energy and environmental intensity of food provided to clients, including starting and promoting community gardens, partnering with local co-ops and farmers (for example, trading food for labor), composting food wastes, and providing nutrition and food preparation skills training, along with teaching of other basic life skills.

Historic preservation organizations. When restoring properties, use recycled building materials and incorporate green building concepts and techniques when they are compatible with preservation constraints. Seek material suppliers and laborers from the local community, use native plant species for landscaping, and use landscape and hardscape in ways that increase occupant comfort while reducing excessive building energy consumption, stormwater runoff, and other adverse impacts.

Hospitals, clinics, and other health care organizations. Consider expanding the vision to focus on wellness from a broad perspective. Focus on overall wellness and personal health among patients and staff, along with awareness that good health includes but is not synonymous with the absence of disease. Ensure that facilities are designed and operated to provide a high level of indoor air quality and to limit transmission of and possible exposure to chemicals and disease-causing microbes. Encourage and provide incentives for care providers and staff to model healthy behavior, and train them to deliver information and guidance on healthy lifestyles to patients and clients. Create or augment existing patient-directed programs to emphasize the importance of complete and balanced nutrition, regular exercise (particularly outdoors), cessation of unhealthy habits (especially smoking and overuse of alcohol), and stress reduction. Encourage consumption of locally grown foods and provide information about them. Raise awareness of exposure to pesticides, other toxic materials, and unhealthy indoor environments (such as structures containing lead paint, mold, or asbestos).

DEVELOPING A SUSTAINABILITY POLICY AND OBJECTIVES

Regardless of how the environment is viewed in the context of your organization's ongoing work, the board should establish or direct the development of an organization-wide environmental, sustainability, or social responsibility policy. This policy is the cornerstone of effective environmental and social programs and establishes the position, aspirations, and commitments of the organization and its members. The absence of a comprehensive, coherent policy has hindered the development of many well-intentioned environmental and sustainability improvement initiatives. To avoid disappointment and optimize resource use, boards should establish a simple, clear statement of principles and commitments regarding the environment and, if they choose, broader issues of social equity and economic development under the rubric of sustainability. For organizations that have one or more existing policies, it is appropriate to review their provisions every few years and make refinements, as appropriate, to reflect operating experience and lessons learned, accommodate new goals and priorities, and address emerging issues and concerns.

Policies should be concise, unambiguous, and written in understandable language. Policy statements may include long-range aspirations and strategic objectives, but it is generally best to leave specific goals and milestones to strategies and tactical plans.

POLICY PROVISIONS

While drafting a sustainability policy may seem intimidating, it does not need to be. A solid, workable policy consisting of a limited number of widely recognized principles and practices is likely to gain the rapid support of the organization's other stakeholders.

- Comply with the law and the organization's own commitments.

- Determine and control the organization's significant environmental and social aspects.

- Prevent pollution at the source where possible.

- Conserve resources where feasible.

- Protect staff, members, and constituents from harm on the job when participating in programs and receiving services.

- Practice nondiscrimination in employment and ongoing professional opportunities.

- Check progress and improve over time.

- Practice transparency and keep constituents and stakeholders informed on the organization's progress on a regular basis.

- Support the protection of internationally recognized human rights, and ensure that the organization is not complicit in human rights abuses.

- Uphold the freedom of association.

- Avoid and prevent all forms of forced, compulsory, and child labor in work performed by or on behalf of the organization.

Note that the last three principles are most relevant outside the United States but also are prominent concerns for U.S.-based organizations that serve people or perform mission-related activities in developing countries.

A policy with these provisions sends a clear signal that the organization understands and accepts responsibility for improving the environment and human well-being and will determine what aspects of its operations, if any, pose significant adverse effects. It ensures that improvement efforts will be evaluated and implemented where they are sensible and cost effective. Such a policy also makes it clear that improved environmental and social performance over time is expected, so that stakeholders know that the organization's board and management recognize and are responsive to the needs and expectations of their community and American society at large.

Rather than overextending the organization or making promises that may be difficult to keep, such a policy helps the organization keep its commitments to funders, members, constituents, staff, and supporters. Nothing about these policy provisions suggests addressing environmental or social issues that an organization does not contribute to or investing resources in reducing or eliminating adverse effects unless doing so is an effective and financially feasible.

Sustainability policies need three other important provisions. First, the policy requirements should apply to all company operations and employees. The purpose of any policy, from the perspective of those who develop and issue it, is to enable (and in some cases enforce) behavioral changes that result in meaningful improvement over time. Policy applied evenly ensures fairness and promotes the collaboration and multidisciplinary cooperation needed to address sustainability issues effectively across the organization.

Second, board oversight is crucial to securing and maintaining support throughout the organization for the investments of time and other resources, as well as the behavioral changes that are required to adopt more sustainable behavior. This support and involvement must remain tangible and visible as the sometimes-difficult work of implementing new ways of doing things proceeds during the crucial early months and years. The simplest and clearest signal of ongoing support that can be sent throughout the organization is that the board is committed to and cares about the work and its ultimate result.

Finally, for an organization to take a full and honest look at its environmental and social footprint, it must consider both upstream and downstream factors: the nature of the materials, goods, and services that it procures and its suppliers' employment and social practices, as well as the energy, environmental, and health and safety aspects of the services it provides to its constituents.

The environmental policy of the diversified industrial firm 3M offers the advantages of brevity and clarity, as well as several unusual features that are worthy of note (Exhibit 3.1). Several provisions reflect the company's culture, history, and values. For example, the statement that 3M will "solve its own environmental and conservation problems" demonstrates that the company, which prides itself on innovation and continually bringing new products to market, believes that understanding and resolving environmental issues are well within its core competencies. In the same fashion, the commitment to "develop products that support a sustainable environment" suggests that 3M views the emerging emphasis on environmental performance as an opportunity rather than a burden.

Although few nonprofits resemble major multinational companies, the 3M example is a reminder that nonprofit boards, when crafting environmental policies, should give careful thought to how environmental and sustainability issues affect and are affected by their organizations and how their unique missions, cultures, and capabilities can be used to address these issues appropriately and effectively. Sample policies from the nonprofit world are provided in the Appendix to this book.

Exhibit 3.1

Applies To	This policy applies to all 3M operations.
Introduction	3M has long recognized the necessity for responsible environmental management and conservation of resources. 3M has also recognized the global nature of environmental matters and the importance of constructive cooperation in achieving international environmental conservation. 3M will continue to demonstrate leadership through our commitment to environmental management and the principles of sustainable development.
Policy Statement	We will continue to recognize and exercise our responsibility to:

- Solve our own environmental and conservation problems.

- Develop products that support a sustainable environment.

- Prevent pollution at the source wherever and whenever possible.

- Conserve natural resources through the use of optimized manufacturing operations, reclamation, and other appropriate methods.

- Assure that our facilities and products are in compliance with applicable national, regional, and local environmental requirements, and in conformance with other applicable environmental obligations.

- Assist, whenever possible, governmental agencies and other official organizations engaged in environmental activities.

- Foster continual improvement through company and employee initiative.

For Further Information	Contact 3M Environmental Operations, St. Paul, Minnesota, 651-778-6442.
Approved By	EHS Committee
Original Issue Date	February 10, 1975
Last Revision Date	April 11, 2008

Source: http://solutions.3m.com/ 3MContentRetrievalAPI/ BlobServlet?locale=en_ US&lmd=1210777195000 &assetId=1180581671127 &assetType=MMM_Image &blobAttribute=ImageFile

Having established the organization's sustainability posture and commitments, the next logical step is to establish a few long-range objectives. These statements are guideposts showing the principal thrusts of environmental and social improvement activities and future points of reference to ensure that progress and overall direction are on track. Objectives should be aspirational, reflect the environmental/sustainability policy and commitments, be focused on the medium to long term, and be challenging but reasonable in scope and rigor. Board members must either lead or be intimately involved in this process. Sustainability objectives can take many forms, and a few examples follow:

- Become carbon-neutral and/or generate zero net waste.

- Reduce the total energy consumed by/on behalf of the organization by X percent.

- Reach and maintain a record of no lost-time injuries to employees on an annual basis.

- Become a recognized sustainability leader among peer organizations.

Next, each significant environmental and social objective should be assigned specific targets. Targets should indicate progress toward the defined objective(s), be specific and quantifiable, and have associated time frames for attainment. For each, the organization, led by the board, should define one or a few performance metrics. These should be measurable, direct (where feasible), representative, understandable to staff and stakeholders, verifiable, responsive to stakeholder concerns, consistent with the defined objectives, and, of course, meaningful. Properly designed and implemented metrics and data collection methods will yield accurate, complete, and comparable results that are useful for decision making and credible inside and outside the organization. Board involvement in establishing goals and measurement processes is important to the overall success of any coherent environmental or sustainability improvement initiative.

ASSESSING ENVIRONMENTAL ASPECTS

A sustainability initiative begins with an environmental aspects analysis, which identifies and assesses your organization's actual environmental and social effects. The board may be involved in conducting the analysis, but its primary role is to provide leadership and oversight while the chief executive and staff carry out specific tasks.

Environmental aspects analysis is a key component of environmental management systems (EMS) used by large and small companies and government organizations around the world. For nonprofit organizations, I advocate expanding the scope to encompass major social equity issues. Aspects analysis consists of three sequential steps:

1. Review all activities, products, and services to learn how they intersect with the environment and whether they might involve health, safety, and/or other social issues.

2. Determine the extent to which the organization has control or influence over each. Set aside those that are outside the organization's control or influence.

3. Define and evaluate the significance of each point of intersection (organization–environment or organization–social issue). At minimum, evaluate these types of intersections:

   • pollutant emissions to air, water, or land

   • solid waste generation

   • land alteration

   • use of natural resources (for example, energy and water)

   • worker health and safety

   • local or community concerns or issues

This deceptively simple yet powerful approach yields a clear (and usually small) set of environmental, human health, and social issues that are the most important for the organization to address. The board uses this issue set to define and establish the organization's long-range sustainability objectives. These objectives become the focal point for all subsequent performance improvement efforts, helping to prevent attention and resources from being diverted to issues that simply don't matter to the organization's sustainability performance.

Given the prominence of the global climate change issue, the board may wish to ask the chief executive to ensure that an analysis is performed specifically to quantify the organization's carbon footprint. More than any other issue, climate change and the contribution individuals and organizations make to this phenomenon are under increasing public scrutiny. Right or wrong, any environmental or sustainability initiative may not be viewed as credible if it does not directly address greenhouse gas (GHG) emissions and their control. Using the results of the environmental aspects analysis, it should be possible to identify activities that use fossil fuels — the principal source of greenhouse gases — and at least a rough idea of the extent of use or consumption (for example, business travel miles per year by travel mode or building space occupied in square feet). Using emission factors and methods obtained from sources such as the U.S. Department of Energy, the U.S. Environmental Protection Agency, and the nonprofit Climate Registry, your organization can construct a simple yet reasonably accurate model (in spreadsheet form) that calculates its carbon footprint. Another tool is the GHG emissions calculators developed by EPA and several other entities. The Center for the Study of Carbon Dioxide and Global Change has a helpful compendium of these methods on its CO_2 Science Web site: www.co2science.org/about/ghgreport/calculators.php.

OVERSEEING INVESTMENTS

Board involvement is essential when it comes to investment policy and oversight. Its fiduciary duty extends to overseeing management of the endowment (if one exists), employee pension or retirement accounts, and other investments. The chief executive and/or the chief financial officer handle day-to-day operations, including working with outside managers, but the board or its investment committee shapes investment policies and decisions. In an effort to align decision making with their missions and values — including their environmental or sustainability goals — more nonprofit organizations are addressing socially responsible investing in their policies.

Fiduciary duty has several important elements, including the obligation to put the account owner's or other beneficiary's interests above one's own and to make prudent decisions that maximize the benefits of the investing activity to the beneficiary. Historically, these duties have been interpreted as limiting investing activities to those that maximize returns given a defined level of risk, or conversely, to minimize risk while attaining at least a stated level of financial return. Under this interpretation, many fiduciaries have taken the position that they are prohibited from considering the environmental (or social) characteristics of firms in which they might invest. This posture has impeded the practice of environmental or, more generally, socially responsible investing (SRI), which makes use of corporate environmental, social, and governance (ESG) data.

During the past several years, two major works of legal research and analysis commissioned by the United Nations have altered interpretations of fiduciary duty in the United States and several other developed countries. The second report, released in 2009, suggests that fiduciaries have an affirmative duty to consider responsible investment strategies, that integrating ESG issues into investment and ownership is part of responsible investment, that such integration is required to manage risk and properly evaluate long-term opportunities, and that ESG issues materially affect both company-level and systemic risk and cannot be ignored by the prudent investor.[1]

The implication is that board members who neglect to consider environmental and relevant social factors when overseeing the management of employee retirement, endowment, or other investment accounts may be subjecting themselves to risks and

[1] UNEP Asset Management Working Group, "Fiduciary Responsibility: Legal and Practical Aspects of Integrating Environmental, Social and Governance Issues into Institutional Investment" 2009, www.unepfi.org/fileadmin/documents/fiduciaryII.pdf.

possibly future legal liability. Boards of nonprofit organizations that offer pensions, retirement plans, and/or other benefits that involve investing funds owned or for the benefit of their employees should be aware of this issue and ensure that the chief executive is also aware.

Portfolio screening, a common tactic in socially responsible investing, involves evaluating investment options based on social, environmental, or responsible governance criteria. Organizations pursuing improved environmental sustainability might consider, for example, companies that are leaders in adopting clean technologies, have effective environmental practices, or do not manufacture products with harmful impacts on the environment or human health. Boards should evaluate existing policies and practices with regard to ESG issues and modify them if necessary. In addition, boards need periodic updates on how investments are being managed with respect to ESG issues.

PROVIDING OVERSIGHT

Change begins at the top. The board is responsible for and involved in establishing the organization's posture toward environmental and sustainability issues. Historically, both corporate and nonprofit boards have not viewed environmental and some social issues as of strategic import, preferring to delegate oversight to management and staff. In recent years, however, this position has begun to change in fundamental ways as the possible organization-wide impacts of global environmental issues such as climate change have become clearer and as shareholders and stakeholders have demanded more extensive and effective environmental and social policies, practices, and disclosure.

Your board can either formally adopt oversight responsibility for the organization's sustainability posture and performance or delegate that responsibility to a task force or committee. This arrangement will provide the necessary clarity of responsibilities and lines of authority and accountability. In addition, it is advisable to assign day-to-day responsibility for implementing the sustainability policy and attaining the associated performance goals to the chief executive or another identified senior staff member.

In this way, your organization can ensure that sustainability issues are led by people who have authority for setting overall direction, establishing objectives, and deploying resources. This approach also signals to interested parties inside and outside the organization that sustainability issues are a board-level concern, treated consistently and strategically across the organization as important mission-related matters.

In addition to having a firm grasp on the multiple roles your board should play in leading a sustainability initiative, you must also understand the variety of opportunities available to pursue environmental improvement across the organization. Chapter 4 reviews the most common opportunities available to nonprofits. It is the board's job to discuss, promote, and support action at the staff level through the chief executive. It is the chief executive's job to lead the staff in day-to-day implementation of the organization's environmental policy and goals.

Chapter 4

Sustainability Across the Organization

For your organization to make substantial and durable gains in its sustainability posture and performance, the board must provide visionary leadership and oversight. This means building a partnership with the chief executive that comes with its governance role, and working together, ensuring that the appropriate structures and processes are put in place to bring about any needed organizational change and drive continual improvement in sustainability performance. While I have great respect for the efficacy and accomplishments of some of the informal networks that have taken form in organizations of all sizes during the past few decades, such approaches are not suitable for pursuing organizational sustainability. Instead, to achieve the organization-scale change required, it is essential to establish clarity regarding how things are going to run, who is in charge and accountable, and what the priorities are.

Boards and individual board members have a vital role in oversight of internal programs to achieve the performance goals defined in the organization's sustainability policy. Equipped with this policy guidance from the board, the chief executive and staff will be able to make the day-to-day decisions about managing the many activities affecting organizational sustainability.

The best way to improve environmental or sustainability performance is to establish programs or retool operations to focus on the issue. It is very important to ensure that such programs explicitly address the activities that create the organization's significant environmental and social aspects. The board and the chief executive will be in a strong position to do so, and to focus on only the most important issues, by reviewing the results of the environmental aspects analysis described in Chapter 3.

Incentives have a powerful effect on the willingness of people to change existing behaviors. Even if behavioral change is relatively simple and painless, it is much more likely to occur if people are motivated out of self-interest to adopt new and preferred practices. Providing appropriate incentives for the behaviors that are required to attain goals is a crucial determinant of success.

Nonprofit organizations that pursue sustainability should ensure that their programs and activities include the following attributes:

- training, as appropriate, particularly in addressing issues such as material use, waste reduction, quality, workplace safety, ergonomics, and wellness

- performance appraisal, including incentive compensation, for responsible managers and executives

- incentives to nonmanagerial employees or teams for meeting organizational goals

As a strong believer in the power and efficiency of markets and in the internal discipline required to manage any enterprise effectively, I believe that any investments made in pursuit of environmental or sustainability performance improvement must be financially tenable and sensible. Objectives, targets, and environmental and/or social issues management programs should include financial data and be expressed in financial terms wherever possible. Having these data enables the organization to make informed decisions about what to do and in what order. This approach is crucial for two reasons:

1. Investing in environmental or social improvements that are noneconomic (i.e., that cost more than the value of the benefits they confer) destroys the capital of the organization. Fundamentally, sustainability involves finding the appropriate balance among environmental health and safety (EHS), social, and economic issues and imperatives. Consistently devoting resources to activities that destroy value undermines the long-term sustainability of the organization.

2. Investing in noneconomic activities to achieve EHS or social improvements leaves less financial capital to pursue other activities that would provide both EHS/social and economic benefits. Consequently, such behavior produces fewer EHS or social benefits than could be produced with a more rational approach. Splashy corporate public relations campaigns touting purchases of (or subsidies for) hybrid vehicles, capital-intensive philanthropic activities, and other sorts of feel-good activities may seem admirable and can

engender positive buzz, but they mask the reality that more could have been accomplished while spending the same amount of money or less.

USING LOGIC MODELING

Applying a formal, logic-driven process is a sound approach to nonprofit sustainability program design activities. This deceptively powerful technique can be of great value to nonprofit boards and staff as they consider new initiatives and evaluate existing programs over time. A logic model (see Exhibit 4.1) is a visual tool that maps the relationships among the results (outcomes) that an organization is seeking to achieve, the resources and activities that it uses or plans to use to attain these outcomes, the outputs of these activities, and the agents (clients) through which decisions or actions will be taken that generate the short-term and longer-term results desired. The logic model and its underlying concepts can enable people to make breakthrough improvements in the ways in which they structure and operate their programs.

Exhibit 4.1

THE LOGIC MODEL

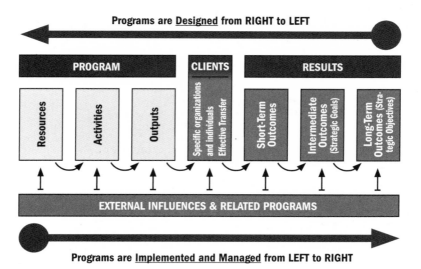

Source: Adapted from "Logic Models: A Tool for Telling Your Program's Performance Story." *Elevation and Program Planning. 1999.*

For example, a community development organization might have the long-term objective of improving the health and social/economic well-being of the people living in a particular neighborhood or area. Medium-term outcomes toward these objectives might include rising employment rates, household incomes; academic performance; and lower mortality, illness, and high school dropout rates, among many others. Short-term outcomes toward these medium-long-term objectives might include reductions in the crime rate and childhood obesity, increases in high school graduation rates, fewer teenage pregnancies, and the like. The clients in this case would be the people living in the community and other local institutions, while the outputs would be delivered services (e.g., specialized educational offerings, home inspections, nutrition counseling, day care, and other assistance). The resources used to develop and provide these services would include the people, funds, building space, materials, etc., used by the organization, while the activities might include establishing a presence in the neighborhood, conducting outreach to influential community members, and setting up an ongoing operation of programs, which could include home renovations/energy efficiency improvements, formation of community gardens, health screening, and many others.

For more information about logic models, see the W.K. Kellogg Foundation's Logic Model Development Guide at www.wkkf.org/knowledge-center/resources/2006/02/WK-Kellogg-Foundation-Logic-Model-Development-Guide.aspx.

KEY PROGRAM ISSUES

BUILDING SPACE

Building energy use is a significant, and often the most important, source of an organization's pollutant emissions. Fortunately, cost-effective improvements can reduce energy consumption and associated emissions. Such improvements also have been shown to increase occupants' comfort, which can enhance productivity and reduce absenteeism. While there may be only limited short-term opportunities to make significant changes to physical space, evaluating lease renewal or searching for new office space provides an opportunity to review building energy and environmental characteristics. A simple but effective method is to draft or revise a building space policy or procedure that adds energy efficiency to the conventional selection criteria, such as unit cost, location, and on-site amenities and services. To reduce your organization's overall environmental footprint, the board and chief executive should also consider whether to focus on locations that would reduce employees' commuting distance and time and stimulate use of public transportation.

TRAVEL

Business travel, including transportation and lodging, can be an organization's most significant environmental aspect, mainly because of the energy and pollution emission intensity of airplanes and, to a lesser degree, cars and trucks. Clearly, the issue's importance hinges on the frequency and typical distance of travel by board members, staff, and constituents or members, as well as the relative need for travel to fulfill the mission. If long-distance travel can be reduced through such techniques as video- and Web-conferencing, the organization can reduce its environmental footprint and likely save money. When out-of-town travel is necessary, train or automobile travel might be an alternative to flying.

Boards should ensure that their organizations have examined the travel issue carefully as part of the environmental aspects analysis and, depending on the significance of the issue, establish policies or guidelines on business travel use and transport modes. Boards should consider their own travel as well. While some state laws may require in-person attendance at board meetings, when possible, boards should consider the feasibility and desirability of convening at least some of their meetings via videoconference.

Another major issue is lodging, particularly for organizations that host or sponsor conferences, seminars, training sessions, and large meetings. Hotels and conference facilities may have substantial environmental aspects, including energy use (space heating, cooling, and hot water), solid waste generation, and water use (landscape maintenance, laundries, swimming pools, and guest use). The large environmental footprint of many hotel and resort facilities has not gone unnoticed, and over the past decade the hospitality industry has made significant strides in making its operations more environmentally sound. There are now a number of associations and programs dedicated specifically to helping hotel properties "green" their operations and provide assistance to meeting hosts and planners that wish to reduce the environmental footprint of their conferences. Some of these tools are identified in the Resources section at the end of this book. Boards and chief executives should evaluate the significance of meeting and conference activities, in light of the results of their environmental aspects analysis and mission-related needs, and determine whether they should establish or modify a meetings policy to incorporate green meeting criteria.

EMPLOYEE COMMUTING

In addition to building location, your organization's policy on time spent in the office or other primary work location affects not only direct environmental aspects (from vehicle miles traveled) but also employee quality of life. In many parts of the country, people expend a staggering amount of time, fuel, patience, and lost productivity sitting in rush hour traffic. Every organization's leadership will need to decide what work arrangements are necessary and appropriate for its staff. It may be possible to institute flexible hours, telecommuting, and other such practices. Such sustainable business behavior can result in a reduced organizational energy and environmental footprint, more highly satisfied and productive employees, and possibly reduced absenteeism and turnover. These are tactical management issues that the chief executive and staff should address, but boards may convey, perhaps through a policy, their support for potential new efforts to capture such win-win opportunities.

LEAD BY EXAMPLE

Good leaders attract followers by walking the walk. Here are some ways that your board can adapt its practices to embrace "green governance." Most of the changes involve the board's responsibility in managing its own workflow and meeting procedures. As a bonus, these suggestions also help save money.

- Using board portals to disseminate board books and other relevant information is an easy way to cut down on paper usage. Postage expenses can also be cut significantly. Using large screens, laptops, or tablets in the meeting room can also help, allowing staff to project the information for easy viewing and to ensure that everybody truly is on the same page.

- Choosing a central location for board meetings can reduce flying time for staff and several board members. Replacing some face-to-face board meetings with virtual meetings may lessen the carbon footprint and cut down logistical expenses tied to board meetings. Teleconferencing and e-mail communication eliminate unproductive travel time for everyone involved. Teleconferences are perfectly acceptable methods for convening most committee meetings, but be sure to check state laws before holding a virtual meeting where board members may need to vote.

- Large boards might re-evaluate the board's size for many reasons, but one of the benefits of downsizing is reducing all meeting costs and enhancing every environmental aspect of a meeting.

EMPLOYEE WELL-BEING

Any thoughtful approach to creating a sustainable organization takes into account the welfare of what makes it function: its employees. Instituting a sustainability initiative provides an opportunity to view employee well-being in more expansive light.

Issues include

- general working conditions (hours and location, personal security, potential acute hazards on the job in or near the building space, office ergonomics, adequate light, ventilation, and temperature regulation)

- employee wellness (health screening and monitoring, personal habits such as dietary intake, tobacco use, and availability of exercise options)

- personal and professional growth (educational opportunities, mentoring, access to management, and decision making)

Research has shown that employers that treat their employees well receive important benefits, many of which have nontrivial financial implications, such as lower absenteeism and turnover, reduced workers' compensation and insurance costs, and higher productivity. To the extent that your organization has not yet considered these issues, a sustainability initiative may provide the necessary impetus to do so.

Another aspect of employee well-being concerns how your organization behaves under unusual circumstances, from personal and family emergencies to large-scale natural or manmade disasters. As part of any sustainability initiative, the board and chief executive should review personnel policies and procedures addressing excused absences, expectations of staff on business travel, and employee responses to emergency conditions. Ensuring that there is clarity around what to do when confronted with challenging circumstances will promote clear thinking and appropriate decision making on the part of employees. Policies and procedures should also make it clear that employees are free to avoid travel to work or work-related activities or to leave if they believe that their safety or that of others in their care is in jeopardy. As a matter of policy, one or two senior staff members should receive basic training in emergency preparedness and first aid, and in the event of an emergency all staff and visitors should be required to follow instructions from these individuals.

Document Management

Recent technical studies have shown that electronic communication, including e-mail, is not as environmentally benign as some might think. Considering the electricity consumed (and the associated pollutant emissions) by personal computers and by various components of the Internet, it turns out that even a single e-mail message has a carbon footprint. Nevertheless, making smart and efficient use of whatever paper is employed will produce some level of environmental benefits and reduce costs. Simple steps such as recycling office paper (and other materials, where appropriate) and using double-sided printing are obvious places to start.

Segregated office paper — paper and cardstock that are not contaminated with food residue or other trash — is a highly sought-after material and commands (under normal market conditions) a positive and substantial market price. It may be possible to generate a small revenue stream from this material rather than pay to have it removed and disposed. Building management will most likely handle paper recycling, so it might be possible to get your building manager to pursue this activity if office paper recycling is not performed at present.

Materials Use

Depending upon the nature and quantities of materials the organization procures and uses, your board may wish to work with the chief executive to ensure that the energy and pollutant intensity, sources, and post-use management of these materials are evaluated and understood. This approach may help alleviate unintended negative consequences of ongoing materials use and provide support to more environmentally benign enterprises. This type of supply chain management is becoming much more prevalent in the corporate sector. For example, Wal-Mart and many of its major consumer goods suppliers, along with some academic institutions, have formed a consortium to study the lifecycle impacts of many common household products and develop supply chain analysis tools.

At a general level, board members may wish to ensure that their organizations are purchasing and using greener products and services when quality, availability, and cost are comparable to existing offerings. Simple examples include the following commonly used materials and products.

OFFICE EQUIPMENT

Electricity consumption as part of routine activities results indirectly in substantial emissions of greenhouse gases and other pollutants. While emissions vary significantly depending on the types of fuels and technologies being used to generate the electricity, it is reasonable to assert that they can be reduced and avoided. In addition to using equipment only when it is needed and powering down nonessential devices at the end of each day, organizations can establish a policy of procuring only energy-efficient office equipment. Boards can establish clear policies that specify purchase of Energy-Star-labeled equipment when possible and thereby position the organization to reduce both its future energy costs and the associated environmental footprint.

Office Paper

As discussed above, there may be some opportunities for boards and chief executives to review the normal activities of their organizations with an eye toward reducing unneeded paper use (for example, printing e-mails and circulating paper memos). Policies can address both disposal and purchase. The purchase of recycled-content paper is a good way to reduce overall environmental impact and support the development of markets that supply such products.

While paper is made from a renewable resource, paper fiber cannot be recycled indefinitely. New fiber (from trees and their components) must be continually added to produce the paper that we need and use. This fact shifts the focus from making the most of what has already been removed from the ambient environment to ensuring that the trees and forests providing the new fiber introduced into paper making are managed in a way that protects the environment and does not impose undesirable social impacts.

Sustainable forest management programs have been developed in recent years and are now in place across much of North America. These programs include labeling and product chain-of-custody provisions, which allow for forest-derived products, including paper, to carry labels that assure the buyer that the product came from sustainably managed forests. Buyers of paper carrying labels from the Sustainable Forestry Initiative (SFI), the Canadian Standards Association (CSA), the Forest Stewardship Council (FSC), and the Programme for Endorsement of Forest Certification Schemes (PEFC) have reasonable assurance that the product and its supply chain have been evaluated and found to reflect sound forest management standards. Boards may wish to consider drafting or modifying a procurement policy to make labeling in accordance with one of these certification systems a purchasing criterion.

Cleaning Products
Many common commercial cleaning products contain ingredients that are corrosive and/or contain volatile solvents and other substances that can cause discomfort and even acute health effects. While most people do not experience ill effects from occasional exposure, others may experience headaches, nausea, and even allergic reactions. To reduce the possibility of such impacts and their severity, boards may want to establish a policy of using, when feasible, only noncorrosive, low-VOC, low-toxicity cleaning products. Antibacterial soap is another product to eliminate, because its use provides negligible incremental health protection benefits and is helping to create a host of new antibiotic-resistant microbes.

Pesticides
This is another issue that, more likely than not, is addressed by a building owner or manager. Depending on various factors — including location, physical condition, and local climate — pests may be only a minor issue or a significant ongoing nuisance or health hazard. For any situation requiring more than the use of window screens or a fly swatter, integrated pest management (IPM) is likely to be the most effective, economical,

and environmentally sound alternative. As the name implies, IPM involves more than spraying some insecticide around the baseboards. In buildings, it involves three basic elements:

1. **Prevention.** IPM concentrates on the resources that pests need to enter or live in a particular area and seeks to identify and eliminate their points of access, shelter, and nourishment. It also continually monitors for pests themselves, so that small infestations don't become large ones.

2. **Least-toxic methods.** IPM aims to minimize both pesticide use and risk through alternate control techniques and by favoring compounds, formulations, and application methods that present the lowest potential hazard to humans and the environment.

3. **Systems approach.** IPM coordinates pest control (including contracts with outside vendors) with all other relevant activities in and around a building, including design and construction, repairs and alterations, cleaning, waste management, and food service.

As circumstances allow, boards and chief executives should take steps to ensure that IPM is used in all facilities. Any reticence that they encounter may be overcome by informing the responsible building owner/manager that IPM has been required in all federal government property since 1996. IPM information and services are widely available. For an example of useful step-by-step guidance that applies to schools, see www.epa.gov/pesticides/ipm/brochure/ipmprograms.htm.

MEASURING AND REPORTING RESULTS

Defining milestones and measuring progress toward their attainment is a necessary component of a drive toward organizational sustainability. Propelling and sustaining such a drive, there should be performance metrics and timetables that reflect meaningful advances in sustainability, are challenging but realistic, and are appropriate to the organization's principal activities and scale. If existing measurement processes are not sufficient to monitor progress, new procedures must be developed and integrated throughout the organization.

In parallel with this activity, it is important to have a robust and effective corrective action process in place. Such a process ensures that good intentions are acted upon, improvement initiatives are carried out effectively, and timely and appropriate course corrections are made. These steps often require an investment of time and other resources, but they are necessary to ensure that the sustainability-driven initiative takes root. When a program that is launched with great enthusiasm does not succeed, the resulting disillusionment can undermine future improvement efforts.

Another key aspect of effective sustainability management is reporting its results. Regular reporting of management actions and performance results gives internal and external stakeholders assurance that environmental and social policies are being carried out, goals are being attained, and the management system is functioning as intended.

The types, formats, content, and timing of reporting should be tailored to the organization. While this may sound simple, in practice it is anything but. Begin with an examination of organizational mission, objectives, and strategy, and include an intense focus on stakeholder concerns. It may be wise to survey or otherwise develop an understanding of the perspectives of each major stakeholder group. Armed with these insights, the board and chief executive can decide how best to address all major concerns and desires and work to develop, organize, and present the relevant information in a way that is clear, informative, and appropriate to its intended audience. Organizations would be well advised to adopt general conformance with widely accepted organizational sustainability reporting guidelines (e.g., the Global Reporting Initiative) in cases in which formal public reporting is indicated.

CONCLUSION

Environmental and broader sustainability issues will remain important for the foreseeable future. Resolving our major challenges in an effective and equitable way requires the participation of all segments of society, as well as informed, rational, and sensible decision making by government, the private sector, nonprofits, and individuals.

Nonprofit organizations have two important roles to play. First, they have an obligation to understand and control their own environmental and social aspects. And second, they have substantial opportunities for leveraging their talents, resources, and programs to enable and empower others to improve the quality of the environment and the health and well-being of their families and communities.

To do their part, however, nonprofits need leadership that only their boards and executive management can provide. Sustainability must be pursued in a coherent, integrated fashion as an extension of the organization's mission, values, culture, and strategy, and examined in that context. It should not be a stand-alone initiative or a tactical effort bolted on to existing programs and practices. Similarly, in crafting sustainability policy, strategy, and goals, the organization must consider its values, culture, capabilities, and resources. It is up to the board, working with the chief executive, to carry out these activities. Quite simply, if a sustainability program is going to happen and be all that it can be, the board will lead it.

While taking on the issue of environmental improvement or sustainability may seem intimidating, two important factors make the job easier. The first — which this book has addressed — is general agreement on the types of issues to be considered in a sustainability program; the appropriate commitments and goals; the management approaches; and the controls, assurance, and reporting practices that are most likely to satisfy both internal and external stakeholders. The second factor is access to a wide variety of information, guidance, and inspiration that is available at no charge. An extensive list of helpful organizations appears in the Resources section at the end of this book.

At the very least, please do not close this book, put it on a shelf, and never think about putting some of the ideas advanced here into action in your own life and in the organizations in which you provide leadership. We are all in this together, and we will not leave a sustainable world for our children unless we all participate and do what we can when we can.

APPENDIX: SAMPLE ENVIRONMENTAL POLICIES

A few examples of environmental policies are listed below, along with a list of things each policy does particularly well. Please note that these samples may not be appropriate for your organization and are presented here only to help guide policy conversations in your boardroom.

SAMPLE #1

Highlights:

- *Investments in energy use and pollution reductions*
- *Work-life balance*
- *Energy use and pollution reductions*
- *Seeking carbon neutrality*
- *Active environmental, social, and governance investing*
- *Explicit weighing of benefits and costs of sustainable choices*
- *Responsible sourcing for supplies*
- *Investment in employees*
- *Quality of work life*

Compton Foundation, San Francisco

Environmental and Social Sustainability Policies

Energy & Transportation
We subsidize public transit costs for commuting staff, as well as Fastrak costs for those traveling from the East Bay, and for hybrid car owners to enable them to access the high occupancy vehicle lane.

We allow staff to flex their hours so that they can avoid traffic congestion insofar as possible, given the requirements of their daily job responsibilities. We apply carbon offsets to all Foundation-related air travel by staff, board members, and guest speakers and Compton Fellows.

Investments
We actively vote our proxies for environmentally and socially responsible corporate policies. We maintain at least 85% of the Compton Foundation endowment in environmentally and socially screened investments. We provide our staff the option of investing in environmentally and socially responsible retirement funds. As shareholders, the Foundation co-signs letters to corporate management requesting more environmentally sustainable practices. Some of the Foundation's investments are program related.

Supplies
We use 100% post-consumer recycled paper, and reuse paper whenever possible. We buy local, organic (or pesticide-free), and fair-trade foods whenever available at or below a 15% price premium. We buy sustainably produced office supplies whenever available at or below a 15% price premium. We purchase 100% biodegradable and nontoxic cleaning supplies.

Staff
We subsidize up to five days of paid volunteer activity at a nonprofit organization for each of our staff every year. We match on a 2:1 basis charitable contributions of $100 or more made by our staff and board members, up to a total of $9,000 per person per year. We subsidize job-related professional and educational development programs for all staff as schedules and budgets permit. We allow our staff to flex their hours in order to fulfill family caregiving responsibilities insofar as possible, given the requirements of their daily job responsibilities.

SAMPLE #2

Highlights:

- *Integration of sustainability thinking into core business processes and activities*

- *Internal and external climate change mitigation*

- *Integration of sustainability with mission*

- *Integration of sustainability into core business processes*

The David and Lucille Packard Foundation, Los Altos, Calif.

Sustainability Statement

Our Commitment to Sustainability

From its inception, The David and Lucile Packard Foundation has been focused on promoting sustainability as part of its grantmaking and day-to-day operations. Our Conservation and Science program directly explores the links between action and ideas to help conserve and protect natural systems in the United States and around the world. From our support of efforts to slow climate change, to our partnerships with organizations to protect and restore threatened species, our grantmaking programs are committed to finding long-term solutions for some of our most vexing environmental problems.

Similarly, our commitment to sustainability extends to our Foundation's operations and to ensuring that we conduct our business in ways that will help promote the conservation of our environment and preserve our resources for generations to come. We believe that we can best serve our grantees and the communities we support by living the values that we espouse in our grantmaking, and by taking steps to minimize our impact on our natural world.

As a result, for many years we have implemented measures that help the Foundation use fewer resources so that we can actively contribute to the health and well-being of our planet. For example, all remodeling projects at the Foundation are completed using sustainable materials, such as 100% cotton insulation made from recycled blue jeans and Forestry Stewardship Council (FSC) certified wood. In addition, office supplies are selected based on sustainability and recycled content.

Meeting AB 32 Standards
California adopted the Global Warming Solutions Act of 2006 (AB 32) to help the state's residents reduce greenhouse gas emissions that contribute to climate change. The goal of AB 32 is to reduce greenhouse gas emissions to 1990 levels by 2020. The Packard Foundation is using AB 32 goals as a benchmark for reducing its own energy consumption, and we have adopted internal measures to help us reduce our carbon output by approximately 30 percent in the next 10 years.

As part of our efforts, we created a Sustainability Task Force composed of Foundation staff volunteers, to study and recommend how our Foundation can be more energy efficient and reduce our carbon footprint. With the leadership of the task force, our staff are increasing their use of public transportation and carpooling to lessen our reliance on individual commuting; utilizing new technologies to replace or reduce their overall travel; converting our paper files into electronic format for better efficiency; and, sharing tips on how to make changes to personal habits to reduce energy use.

Another part of our sustainability efforts has involved working in partnership with our local community to find common solutions. Our staff volunteer their time with local community groups and actively promote energy-saving measures among local community leaders.

We will continue to look for ways to share our experiences and to learn from others so that we all may improve our sustainability efforts and make long-lasting contributions to our communities and the world we live in.

SAMPLE #3

Highlights:

- *Integration of sustainability with mission*
- *Integration of sustainability into core business processes*
- *Assessment and control of significant aspects*

Madison Children's Museum, Madison, Wis.

Sustainability Mission
At Madison Children's Museum we focus on children, including their future. We are committed to being a sustainable organization, balancing economic, social, and environmental factors to help ensure that we meet our present needs, while enabling future generations to meet their needs. We empower and equip children to actively shape the world they will inherit.

As educational and community leaders, we will

- integrate the principles of sustainability into all major business decisions.
- seek strategic collaborations.
- evaluate and reduce the environmental impacts of our operations.
- design and develop our products, services, and materials with the long-term health of our children and community in mind.

SAMPLE #4

Highlights:

- *Aspiration of leadership*

- *Beyond-compliance commitment*

- *Goal of magnifying impact of sustainability activities*

- *Integration of sustainability with mission*

- *Commitments to stakeholder input, transparency, monitoring, and measurement*

National Maritime Museum, Greenwich, London, United Kingdom

Sustainability Policy Statement

In this statement the term "sustainability" includes the natural, built, economic, and social environments of the National Maritime Museum.

The Museum recognizes its sustainability obligations to its staff, visitors, communities, and stakeholders — both locally and globally — and to present and succeeding generations.

The Museum aims to take a leading role in defining best sustainability practice, and will set its own appropriate and demanding standards where none exist.

The Museum is committed to implementing the requirements of all relevant sustainability legislation and regulations and, where possible, exceeding any relevant minimum requirements.

The Museum will manage activities over which it has control and which impact upon its various "environments" in accordance with the principles of sustainable development.

The Museum aims to raise the sustainability awareness of its staff, visitors, communities, and stakeholders by promoting the concept of sustainable development and by openly recognizing the on-going need to move towards a more sustainable future.

The Museum will monitor its use of natural resources, both non-renewable and renewable, and maximize the efficiency and effectiveness with which they are used, with a view to minimizing environmental impacts.

The Museum will foster and promote research and education in sustainability — for visitors, within its communities and via conferences, publications, and collaborative work.

The Museum will provide appropriate sustainability training and development for its staff, and will encourage them to apply sound sustainability practices at work, at home, and within the wider community.

The Museum is committed to transparency in, and public access to, the formulation and implementation of its Sustainability Policy and objectives. The Museum will formulate, publish, implement, and monitor objectives set out in the overall Policy, and will periodically review their efficiency and promote their continued development.

The Sustainability Policy of the National Maritime Museum will be applicable to all its activities and across all its sites.

RESOURCES

WHERE TO GO FOR INFORMATION, ASSISTANCE, AND INSPIRATION

Sustainability issues are numerous and often complex. Fortunately, there are many valuable sources of information, perspective, tools, and techniques that can reduce the time needed to learn about sustainability and develop the internal practices needed.

INTERNATIONAL STANDARDS AND GUIDELINES

Useful information from international organizations involved in the environmental, health and safety, social equity, and sustainability arenas to guide environmental or sustainability program formation and ensure that new activities are performed in accordance with globally accepted practices.

International Organization for Standardization (ISO)
www.iso.org/iso/home.html

ISO works with business, industry, governments, and other parties to establish common technical definitions and standards to facilitate trade and the transfer of technology. Its standards, guidelines, and related documents provide widely accepted approaches for understanding and managing an organization's environmental and social issues. ISO has issued quality management standards (ISO 9000 series); environmental standards and guidelines (ISO 14000 series), which address such topics as environmental management systems, product labeling, lifecycle analysis, and greenhouse gas accounting; social responsibility guidelines (ISO 26000); and has just issued a new energy management system standard (ISO 50001).

United Nations Environment Programme (UNEP)
www.unep.org (UNEP)
www.unepfi.org (UNEP-FI)

UNEP's areas of interest include climate change, disasters and conflicts, ecosystem management, environmental governance, harmful substances, and resource efficiency. Publications address such topics as building a green economy and poverty eradication, sustainable coastal tourism, and business and biodiversity. UNEP also has convened or supports prominent scientific advisory groups, including the Intergovernmental Panel on Climate Change, and the Ecosystem Conservation Group. It also participates in the UNEP Finance Initiative (UNEP-FI), a global partnership with the financial sector that seeks to understand the impacts of environmental and social considerations on financial performance.

United Nations Global Compact (UNGC)
www.unglobalcompact.org

The United Nations Global Compact, a policy initiative focused on multinational corporations, works with businesses that are committed to aligning their operations and strategies with 10 universally accepted principles in human rights, labor, environment, and anticorruption. The principles may be of particular interest to nonprofit organizations seeking to define appropriate policy commitments.

U.S. GOVERNMENT POLICIES, GUIDELINES, AND OTHER INFORMATION SOURCES

In addition to promulgating regulations, federal agencies focus increasingly on technical assistance, training, information development and dissemination, and other activities intended to move American business and other organizations to beyond-compliance, sustainability-driven behavior.

EXECUTIVE ORDERS

The federal government also leads by example, most often through executive orders signed by the president that require, with any stipulated exceptions, all federal departments, agencies, and locations to conduct their operations in a certain manner or to carry out certain activities. Some executive orders are worth reviewing, because they provide tangible descriptions of how an organization can better understand its current environmental/ sustainability footprint, and then take steps to reduce it. Executive orders can be retrieved, by number, from the National Archives, www.archives.gov/federal-register/executive-orders. Relevant examples include:

- EO 13514, Federal Leadership in Environmental, Energy, and Economic Performance (2009): Establishes sustainability policy and performance improvements of all federal agencies, including improving energy efficiency; measuring, reporting, and reducing greenhouse gas emissions; conserving and protecting water resources; reducing waste and increasing recycling; leveraging purchasing power to promote markets for sustainable technologies and environmentally preferable materials, products, and services; improving the performance and sustainability of federal buildings; accounting for and considering all relevant economic, social, and environmental benefits and costs when making decisions and setting priorities; and reporting annually on their actions and performance, including on public Web sites. This executive order provides, in one place, a relatively complete model for the types of goals and activities an organization might want to consider in developing its own sustainability program.

- EO 13148: Greening the Government through Leadership in Environmental Management (2000): This order broke some new ground by identifying issues and establishing goals, and by requiring federal agencies to use emerging best practices, such as integrating environmental accountability into decisions, environmental management systems, and environmental compliance audit programs and policies that emphasize pollution prevention. It also required agencies to reduce, where cost effective, releases of toxic chemicals by at least 10 percent annually; reduce emissions of ozone-depleting substances; and apply environmentally and economically beneficial landscaping practices.

- EO 12856, Federal Compliance with Right-to-Know Laws and Pollution Prevention Requirements (1993): Required compliance with pollution prevention and emergency planning and community right-to-know provisions established in implementing regulations issued pursuant to EPCRA and the Pollution Prevention Act of 1992.

- EO 12898, Federal Actions to Address Environmental Justice in Minority Populations and Low-Income Populations (1994): Required agencies to make achieving environmental justice part of their missions by identifying and addressing disproportionately high and adverse human health or environmental effects of its activities on minority and low-income populations.

FEDERAL AGENCIES

There are many pockets of expertise and information on environmental and social issues and how organizations can manage them. Key resources include the following:

Environmental Protection Agency (EPA)
www.epa.gov

Charged with implementing major environmental statutes, EPA is a vast repository of information on environmental and human health issues. It provides extensive information on the human health and environmental effects of chemicals and other substances; permissible standards and guidelines for safe exposure; guidance for managing environmental issues and challenges (much of it oriented toward small businesses); tools for organizations and individuals (for example, a personal greenhouse gas emissions calculator); and contacts who can answer questions.

Occupational Safety and Health Administration (OSHA)
www.osha.gov

Provides extensive information on managing hazards in the workplace. While its focus is industrial settings in which such hazards are common (and may be impossible to eliminate), OSHA also has resources of value to nonprofit organizations, including data and statistics; training; guidance manuals, presentations, and posters; and even a training grants program open to nonprofit entities. The information and resources pertaining to workplace ergonomics and common hazards are likely to be of most interest to readers of this book.

General Services Administration, Public Buildings Service (PBS)
www.gsa.gov/portal/content/104444

Owns and operates a portfolio of nearly 10,000 federal buildings across the country, making it one of the largest commercial-style real estate management organizations in the nation. PBS has pioneered the use of energy efficiency and green building design and construction techniques in commercial buildings and has well-developed expertise in green leasing, integrated pest management, indoor environmental quality, and other aspects of designing and operating green building space. It also offers a free sustainable facilities tool (www.sftool.org) with basic information, questions, checklists, and criteria for those wishing to evaluate new building space options.

ENVIRONMENTAL AND SUSTAINABILITY NONGOVERNMENTAL ORGANIZATIONS

These organizations focus on developing and promoting greater understanding of and workable solutions to major environmental and sustainability issues. Some are led by people and organizations from industry, some represent the environmental community, and some have elements of each. Some of the more interesting and relevant among them include the following:

World Business Council for Sustainable Development (WBCSD)
www.wbcsd.org

This global association provides a platform for about 200 companies in 20 major industrial sectors to explore sustainable development, share knowledge, experiences, and best practices, and advocate business positions on these issues. WBCSD publishes insightful reports that address major environmental and sustainability issues, written for readers without advanced technical knowledge.

Business for Social Responsibility (BSR)
www.bsr.org

Global network of more than 250 member companies focused on developing sustainable business strategies and solutions through consulting, research, and cross-sector collaboration. While its purpose and major activities are based more on a consultancy model than those of WBCSD, BSR does provide numerous opportunities for member interaction and has produced a number of reports addressing important sustainability topics.

Global Environmental Management Initiative (GEMI)
www.gemi.org

A consortium of 24 member companies from more than 12 business sectors that provides a forum for corporate environmental managers and directors. GEMI produces useful tools, guidance documents, and other materials to help its members and others understand and actively manage their environmental, health, and safety issues. Of interest to the nonprofit community are downloadable tools addressing sustainable development, performance metrics, strategies addressing water, and managing the environmental health and safety aspects of the supply chain.

World Resources Institute (WRI)
www.wri.org

Global environmental think tank that conducts research; convenes working groups; develops and tests new concepts and frameworks; and generates tools, documents, and other resources. WRI is known for innovative approaches to issues and tools and methods that reflect practical realities. Publications include an array of reports and other resources.

Global Reporting Initiative (GRI)
www.gri.org

An international membership organization that promotes sustainability reporting by corporations and other organizations. GRI's sustainability reporting guidelines, issued for 13 years and now in their third edition, address the three pillars of sustainability: environmental, social equity, and economic. They emphasize labor rights and the interests of organized labor generally. In 2010, 164 U.S. organizations submitted GRI reports; the worldwide total was 1,485. Nonetheless, the GRI guidelines are the de facto global standard for sustainability reporting. Any nonprofit interested in publicly disclosing its sustainability posture and performance should take a close look at the GRI framework and guidelines.

GREEN MEETING ORGANIZATIONS

Three prominent organizations help those involved in the hospitality and tourism industries (on both the supplier and the user sides) green their meetings. The first two are endorsed by the EPA, and the third is organized and sponsored by UNEP and other UN components.

Green Meeting Industry Council (GMIC)
www.greenmeetings.info

An umbrella organization focused on improving the sustainability of the meetings and events industry through education, research, and development of policy and standards. Its members include several major hotel chains, their product and service providers, and the tourism bureaus of several major conference and travel destinations. GMIC publishes downloadable guidance documents on greening a meeting and extensive links to green meeting standards, guidelines, news, and other information.

BlueGreen Meetings
www.bluegreenmeetings.org

Helps meeting planners make environmentally sound decisions, with a Web site that provides tips, checklists, case studies, and other resources designed to make the process simple and save time and money. BlueGreen Meetings is a program of the Oceans Blue Foundation.

Global Sustainable Tourism Council
www.new.gstcouncil.org

Global initiative dedicated to promoting sustainable tourism practices while ensuring tourism that meets its potential as a tool for alleviating poverty. The Global Sustainable Tourism Criteria, a set of 39 standards developed by a coalition of more than 50 organizations, are of particular interest to any nonprofit that convenes or is involved in hosting meetings or conferences in developing countries or in or near sensitive environments.

OTHER RESOURCES

Many educational institutions, federal agencies, and research organizations offer valuable resources ranging from courses on green building and pollution prevention, to published research on environmental attributes of products, to methods and tools for measuring a personal or organizational carbon footprint.

EDUCATIONAL INSTITUTIONS

A variety of classroom and online courses, training materials, and other educational resources address many facets of environmental compliance and management, health and safety, social issues, and sustainability. Virtually every state has educational institutions that provide such offerings. Community colleges tend to focus on hands-on skill development (such as EHS auditing, pollution prevention, and management systems implementation), while universities may offer seminars and short courses in addition to formal degree programs and courses. Nonprofit leaders may wish take advantage of these resources, or empower selected staff to do so.

STANDARDS, GUIDELINES, AND APPROACHES

U.S. Federal Trade Commission (FTC)
www.ftc.gov

Among other activities, regulates consumer advertising, including environmental claims.

U.S. Department of Energy (DOE)
www.doe.gov

Performs research on energy efficiency, alternative energy, and a variety of other environmentally related topics and co-administers (with EPA) the EnergyStar® program.

American National Standards Institute (ANSI)
www.ansi.org

Officially represents the United States in activities of the International Organization for Standardization (ISO), a network of national standards institutes that forms a bridge between the public and private sectors.

ORGANIZATIONAL SUSTAINABILITY

B Corporation
www.bcorporation.net

A relatively new nonprofit organization that advocates a rethinking and restructuring of the purposes of the modern corporation in favor of a model based on social goals as well as profitability. Has developed a rating system and questionnaire that highlights many issues of interest in improving environmental/sustainability performance. `

Environmental Defense Fund
www.edf.org

Environmental nonprofit that, among other activities, has operated partnership programs with businesses and other organizations seeking to improve their environmental performance.

SUSTAINABILITY PUBLICATIONS AND WEB SITES

The following Web sites and electronic newsletters provide a steady stream of information and commentary addressing aspects of sustainability.

Corporate EcoForum
www.corporateecoforum.com

A membership organization representing corporate environmental, health and safety, and sustainability professionals. Publishes informative weekly e-newsletter and occasional research reports.

Environmental Leader
www.environmentalleader.com

A daily trade publication oriented toward the business community and focusing on energy, environmental, and sustainability news.

GreenBiz
www.GreenBiz.com

A group of Web sites addressing greener design, information technology, business, and buildings, as well as responses to climate change. Many have free electronic newsletters.

Sustainable Business
www.sustainablebusiness.com

Environmental news, green jobs, and green investing information.

ORGANIZATIONS

American Forest and Paper Association, www.afandpa.org

American Tree Farm System, www.treefarmsystem.org

Canadian Standards Association International, www.csa-international.org

Center for a New American Dream, www.newdream.org

Coalition for Environmentally Responsible Economies, www.ceres.org

Food and Agriculture Organization of the United Nations, www.fao.org

Forest Stewardship Council–International, www.fscoax.org

Forest Stewardship Council–United States, www.fscus.org

GreenBlue, www.greenblue.org

Keep America Beautiful, www.kab.org

The Montreal Process, www.mpci.org

National Recycling Coalition, www.nrcrecycles.org

NatureServe, www.natureserve.org

Paper Recycling Association, www.pppc.org

Programme for the Endorsement of Forest Certification Schemes, www.pefc.org

Sustainable Forestry Initiative, www.sfiprogram.org

UN Economic Commission for Europe, Timber Committee, www.unece.org/forests

U.S. Bureau of Transportation Statistics, www.bts.gov

U.S. Energy Information Administration, Department of Energy, www.eia.gov

U.S. Forest Service, Department of Agriculture, www.fs.fed.us

U.S. Postal Service, www.usps.com

ABOUT THE AUTHOR

Peter A. Soyka is a prominent environmental management and strategy consultant, and the founder and president of Soyka & Company, LLC, a small consultancy focused on illuminating and resolving the issues limiting sustainable business success. With more than 24 years of environmental management experience, he has served a wide variety of private, public, and nonprofit sector clients focusing on improved, cost-effective environmental and sustainability performance. Much of Mr. Soyka's recent work has involved identifying and capturing the financial and other organizational benefits of proactive environmental management and sustainability practices.

During his career, Mr. Soyka has successfully designed and executed hundreds of consulting projects, including a number devoted to driving sustainability thinking and practices into client organizations at a strategic level. He also has developed a substantial number of new research findings, methods, tools, and analytical approaches, and other innovations for understanding and acting upon the organizational and financial aspects of corporate sustainability issues. He is particularly well known for his pioneering work at the intersection of environmental management/sustainability and finance, and has authored several path-breaking empirical and survey research studies exploring various dimensions of this topic. Mr. Soyka also has served in executive positions in several national-scale, publicly traded consulting/engineering firms, through which he developed an in-depth understanding of the workings of and pressures within large corporate organizations, and the challenges inherent in bringing constructive change to such entities. The diversity of Mr. Soyka's work and clientele over the years provides him with perspective on the range of views held within the corporate/trade association, regulatory, and nonprofit communities. Accordingly, he offers a good sense, from the "front lines," of what the important environmental and broader sustainability issues and challenges are, how they can be resolved or managed, what barriers may be encountered, and how they can effectively be overcome.

Mr. Soyka has been a featured invited speaker at a number of national and international environmental management conferences and symposia, and has participated in workshops and taught courses on such topics as corporate finance and governance, environmental accounting, pollution prevention, and environmental performance/sustainability indicators. He has authored scores of published journal articles, book chapters, guidance and training manuals, feasibility studies, technical background documents, multi-volume reports to Congress, regulatory impact analyses, and other works.

Mr. Soyka holds Master of Environmental Management and Master of Business Administration degrees from Duke University and a Bachelor of Arts degree in Zoology and Environmental Studies from the University of Vermont.